FASTER
SAFER
WEALTHIER

www.gregbott.com
ISBN: 978-1-7778132-0-8 (print)
ISBN: 978-1-7778132-1-5 (ebook)
Ordering Information:
Special discounts are available on quantity purchases by corporations, associations, and others. For details, contact us at www.gregbott.com.

Contents

Systems for Scaling Wealth

Take Ownership and Start Building Wealth Today

FASTER
SAFER
WEALTHIER

SKIP THE START-UP AND BUY
A STABLE BUSINESS TO BUILD
INTERGENERATIONAL WEALTH

DR. GREGORY BOTT

AN ENTREPRENEUR'S JOURNEY
(TO WEALTH)

Why Entrepreneurship? Why Now?

On a Thursday in August, our team braced for the worst—we had just tripled the size of our company overnight. Would we be able to keep up with the phone calls and emails in the days, weeks, and months to follow? Had we taken on more than we could handle?

We had just purchased the business of a competitor. Leading up to the closing date, the team could feel my anxiety as I nervously managed by pacing around the office, continually asking for reassurance that every department was ready to take on the added workload. However, as we anxiously coached our teams through the process and provided for repetitive training on our systems, the phones never rang. It was the calm before the storm, but the storm never came.

What were we overlooking? Was it really that easy? At the stroke of midnight, we had just achieved a revenue growth that was twice that of which we had been able to accomplish in our start-up grind during the past two and a half years.

Prior to this, my experience had been with start-ups, not the acquisition of an existing business. What I had failed to recognize is that we had purchased a complete business: the customers, the talented staff, and the refined systems. Every detail of the business continued as a well-oiled machine.

After an anticlimactic week of business as usual, I looked up at my business partner through the glass that separates our offices, closed my laptop, and yelled out, "You seem to have this under control. I'm going farming. See you in November."

They didn't need me. I would just be in the way of people far more talented than myself. I could continue to collect my paycheque, while once again taking control of my most valuable resource—my time: time to be where I want, when I want, and not to be reliant on performing a certain work function at a certain time in exchange for a paystub. Time to read, write, research, teach, travel—or farm.

What areas of your life do you wish to have more time for? Try to imagine your life one year from now—you are the owner of a well-established business, which is producing your goal income, and you are on pace to hit personal financial freedom that ultimately results in the lifestyle you have always dreamt of. Is that possible?

There has never been a better time to be an entrepreneur; to own a business and to grow that business, with the outcome of building and retaining substantial wealth at a level unachievable in a nine-to-five career. And it has never been easier to build sustainable intergenerational wealth within a single generation.

A recent study found that nearly nine out of 10 millionaires in America have made their own wealth: "… they started with nothing, and in many cases came from extreme poverty" (Cumberland 2019, 20). An individual's economic starting point has therefore become less relevant to where they end up on the financial spectrum.

During previous economic periods, wealth tended to be inherited between generations, and it continued to accumulate through investments, either in private or public corporations or in real estate. It was the landowners and, later, the factory owners who held the abundance of wealth. As a result, the fortunes of the superrich tended to come from inherited wealth—the passing of capital between generations.

However, in the current economic climate, new money prevails. Salaries and active business incomes account for the majority of the income of the superrich (e.g. the top one percent of income earners), who are now termed "the working rich" (Freeland 2012). We are in an economic period of fresh opportunity: a period in which becoming financially whole is achievable for almost anyone and where opportunities are waiting to be captured by those enthusiastic about engaging with the entrepreneurial grind.

The exit of the baby boomers is opening up gaps in business ownership, making it easy to find opportunities. The pace of technological change provides an unprecedented opportunity for growth. A skilled and transient workforce is looking for purpose, and investors are idly standing by with an abundance of capital, waiting for you to convince them that your proposed investment is the right fit for them.

Through technology and globalized distribution channels, entrepreneurs can create wealth at an exponential rate that previous generations could only have dreamt of. Digital marketing alone has allowed organizations to become global companies overnight, no longer reliant on clunky and expensive traditional advertising mechanisms, often narrowly focused on and capable only of building local brand exposure.

All of the fundamentals have come together for building wealth through business ownership and in an exponentially shortened time frame.

Business Ownership as a Pathway to Success

Entrepreneurship can be a conduit to the achievement of success, however you choose to define it. For many, success can be defined as "… the ability to live your life the way you want to live it, doing what you most enjoy, surrounded by people you admire and respect" (Tracy 2017, xv).

Everyone has their own objectives with entrepreneurship, whether they be income and wealth, freedom and flexibility, social change, or all of the above. It is important to reflect on why you want to be an entrepreneur.

Do you feel that you have a strong ability to operate a company? Are you looking to be financially whole and complete? Do you want to give your children opportunities to travel and to go to the university of their choosing or to ensure that the best medical treatment will be available if someone close to you becomes ill? Do you have a compelling vision to make the world a better place? Are you an effective team builder?

These are all good reasons to become an entrepreneur. For me, the reasons are multifaceted, but most prominent among them are the challenge, the ability to be a positive influence on team members who partake in this journey alongside me, a sense of purpose, and the opportunity to be able to positively give back to the community in terms of time, knowledge, and resources.

Entrepreneurship through acquisition can be a gateway to taking ownership of your time. Ownership of your time is the freedom to be where you want to be, when you want to be there. It is the freedom to choose to spend your time on what brings the most value to your life.

But entrepreneurship is not for everyone. Financial swings and uncertainties can place pressures on relationships, marriages, and finances. Such pressures frequently (although often unspoken) exacerbate mental health challenges. When reading biographies of the rich, it seems more the norm than the exception that authors feel the need to dedicate significant sections of text to past periods of financial hardship—phases of ramen noodles, basement offices, divorce, and bankruptcy.

Arlene Dickinson is a successful Canadian entrepreneur and the owner of Venture Communications and District Ventures Capital, a venture capital fund. She is a panellist on the television show *Dragon's Den* where aspiring entrepreneurs pitch their business concepts to a panel of wealthy entrepreneurs. In her book, *All In*, Dickinson comments, "I have witnessed first-hand the hazards of trying to embrace the entrepreneurial lifestyle without the inner strength to underwrite it. From addiction and broken relationships to failed businesses and bankruptcy, the personal toll of the entrepreneurial life can be devastating ..." (Dickinson 2013, 4).

There is only one guarantee as an entrepreneur, and this is that you will have setbacks along this nonlinear journey. Your story might not be one of rags to riches, but it is guaranteed to be one of ups and downs.

The reality is that most businesses do not survive and that most business owners who do stick with it make less than they would have had they continued to work as an employee in their prior career. This can be prevented.

Entrepreneurship is messy, complex, paradoxical, and emotional. But an alignment of your business practices with principles of wealth creation and retention can prepare you for your journey.

I do believe that with a business acquisition, these unfortunate detours can be avoided or at least mitigated through a combination of research (learning from and reading about others who have been there) and by surrounding yourself with strong partnerships and mentors who are capable of filling in any gaps in your personal capabilities. Most of the risks inherent with start-ups are not inherent in an acquisition. I therefore feel an obligation to share with you the benefits of business acquisition over the start-up and to share elements of my personal journey with you—both the ups and the downs.

Is this ride something that you have the stamina for?

Don't Drink the Kool-Aid in the Headlines

Although business ownership can be a conduit to achieving your personal definition of success, most business owners, even seasoned entrepreneurs, fail to elevate their businesses—and thus their lives—in any meaningful way. Most of what we read and hear about entrepreneurship is inaccurate or fixated on outliers—the young and charismatic billionaire, for example—which leads aspiring entrepreneurs on a rudderless journey, chasing a facade.

However, the typical entrepreneur is not the young risk taker who developed a revolutionary software in their parents' basement. "In fact, the romanticized narrative of the young, mostly male, high-tech wizard accounts for the smallest constellation in the universe of entrepreneurs—only about five to seven percent" (Schramm 2018, 1). A successful everyday entrepreneur is more likely to own and operate a midsized business after a series of career experiences that they are able to build upon.

And most do not start off wealthy. In a study of successful entrepreneurs through business acquisition, Harvard professors Richard Ruback and Royce Yudkoff found that "none had bought a business before or had significant personal wealth when they started, and all of them raised money from investors to complete their acquisitions" (2017, 5). It was the company that made them wealthy over time.

The business media's attention focuses almost exclusively on multinational companies, which has thrust a perception onto the public that the founders of Uber, Alibaba, Virgin, Apple, or Tesla represent the standard typecast of an entrepreneur. Such stories have further created a fixation on the lure of the start-up, overlooking acquisition as an alternative opportunity. Richard Branson (Virgin), Sarah Blakely (Spanx), and Elon Musk (Tesla, SpaceX), among others, have become superheroes to aspiring business graduates.

The issue with start-ups is that they do not provide a palatable risk-reward trade-off, leading to their high failure rate. Despite their perceived appeal, it is often overlooked "that unicorn companies are more anecdotal than typical" (Deibel 2018, 15).

Mainstream business books and self-help gurus have followed suit, preying on those easily influenced by charismatic speakers. Such business literature has thus become gimmicky; the proverbial used car salesmen of the past have moved online, selling get-rich-quick schemes disguised as coursework and conferences, promising that you, too, will be rich if you follow these "five simple steps." Such shortcuts have somehow taken precedent over work ethic, perseverance, life experience, and incremental gains on your journey toward compounding wealth.

Too often, offices are engulfed with overly enthusiastic individuals, fresh off a Tony Robbins or Grant Cardone weekend seminar. Such self-help gurus have made millions off their coursework and conferences and have cult-like followings. Having taken a sip of the cultic Kool-Aid, these followers are convinced that if they follow such easy steps, they, too, will end up living next door to Elon Musk, basking in the sun on Richard Branson's private island, and swimming in their money-filled pool like Scrooge McDuck.

Although there is a place for such coaching and value in dreaming big, such narratives provide little insight into who entrepreneurs really are and what they actually do. This fixation on the superrich has left everyday entrepreneurs invisible, causing them to fall off the radar as role models to would-be business owners.

In this book, I provide a more realistic peek behind the curtain and a healthier articulation of what it means to be an entrepreneur. This comes not only from a more structured understanding of who an everyday entrepreneur is but also, and more importantly, a perspective on how to more realistically achieve and maintain wealth through business ownership.

The opportunities waiting for an entrepreneur's energy are endless. But before acquiring a business, you must be clear about your personal and professional objectives and take a realistic and reflective inventory of your personal skills and abilities. You must be able to articulate your passions and your purpose.

For many people, entrepreneurship is about financial freedom upon retirement. But it can be more than that; it can be financial freedom *during* your working tenure, not just in preparation for retirement. It is important to enjoy the journey itself, not just the end. It will be a miserable tenure if you do not embrace the journey.

Why Am I Telling You This?

At the age of 24, I quit my full-time corporate employment in pursuit of both higher education and entrepreneurship. Over the past number of years, I have owned and operated numerous businesses across multiple industries, including hospitality, real estate, and agriculture. These businesses have ranged from franchised to independent, from start-ups to acquisitions, from heavily regulated to the Wild West, from having numerous layers of staffing to one-person operations, from being heavily leveraged to having no debt, and from sole ownership to having numerous shareholders.

I have found this journey to be quite rewarding. Some of the most impactful achievements for me have been the numerous tangible examples of providing meaningful employment and mentorship—being a role model and helping people achieve their own success.

Small-business ownership has also afforded me the opportunity to prioritize my life around outcomes that are unrelated to my employment or the daily grind. Entrepreneurship has allowed me to travel, to undertake academic programs across three continents, to sit on nonprofit boards, and the flexibility to continue a passion for writing.

But my journey has been far from linear. I started by jumping in headfirst and only more recently made the journey one of learning and discovery. There were many things that went well and a number of outcomes that did not go well. The latter provided me an opportunity for reflection and the opportunity to approach similar situations differently on my next go around.

I wish that I had better understood the relationship between business acquisitions and wealth accumulation, and, more importantly, wealth retention earlier in my entrepreneurial journey, as a naïve gravitation toward the start-up has made for significant swings in wealth and emotions.

Such swings did, however, give me the chance to reflect and develop a more purposeful approach. I now have a solid foundation of principles that I rely upon as I approach business ownership and personal finances. My decisions are now more intentional and measured against such principles. Many of such principles provide the foundation for this book.

Between Broke and Billionaire

This book is for those interested in the inner workings of small- to medium-sized businesses. I do not pull any punches in outlining the bad along with the good—as I have certainly had my share of both. Perhaps you are interested in starting your first business. Maybe you are contemplating between establishing a start-up or purchasing an existing business. Or maybe you are a seasoned entrepreneur and business owner who is considering growth through acquisition.

I provide a more realistic account of entrepreneurship from inside the trenches. Although I have had my fair share of wins and continue to choose entrepreneurship over employment every day, I will also share with you the many struggles that I have encountered—those small anecdotes in one's journey that contribute to the journey more than we initially realize. Others are more stressful happenings, like the short period of time during which my net worth dropped by a half a million and the sleepless nights I spent wondering how I was going to fund the upcoming payroll.

While there is a plethora of books on entrepreneurship and business acquisition, they mostly tend to start with the assumption that the reader has a once-in-a-lifetime innovation and a one-track objective of being a billionaire.

Although such audacious goals are admirable, books about the 0.01 percent of income earners are not overly helpful in providing clarity to the inner workings of the everyday entrepreneur; rather, they encourage a swing-for-the-fences mentality and an increased risk tolerance, ultimately contributing to the high statistics of business failures.

Sure, such literature may be inspirational, and there is an obvious value in studying the habits of the elite, but by no means do such narratives provide a comprehensive playbook for the everyday entrepreneur. A more honest answer to how the wealthy become wealthy is through a story of a slow and methodical grind.

It is not necessary to be in the billionaire tax bracket to live a full life and to feel financially whole. How much do you require to achieve your desired lifestyle?

There is a space between broke and billionaire. And there is a space between a side hustle and a billion-dollar empire. Discover, acquire, and occupy your space.

In this space, there are thousands of entrepreneurs meeting everyday consumer and business requirements. These everyday millionaires own and operate everyday companies: construction, paving, equipment or automotive dealerships, real estate development, manufacturing, marketing, and digital media.

One prominent entrepreneur I know prepared in a very purposeful way. He had wanted to own a business and had heard that the local equipment dealership was to come up for sale. So, he applied to work there as a mechanic. Over time, he bought the dealership and owned it for the next 37 years.

Business ownership helped him build up a significant commercial real estate portfolio and become an important contributor to the community. This isn't a headline grabbing story, yet it fundamentally changed the way his family is able to live, where they vacation, and what resources were available to them when someone in the family became ill.

I've organized the chapters in this book to help prepare you for your journey. Given the importance of first reflecting on where you currently are in your journey and where you would like to go, I start by walking you through a reflection on your purpose, skills, and abilities. Then, armed with a clearer understanding of your starting point, we'll examine whether a start-up or an acquisition will be the more prosperous journey for you (hint—a thorough examination usually favours the acquisition).

I provide a practical guide to help you build the capacity required to achieve success. You will form a greater appreciation for the critical aspects of entrepreneurship, such as selecting the right industry and business for you and choosing between establishing a start-up and acquiring an existing business. After such analysis, you will learn about the process involved in acquiring a business, from selection and negotiation through to operations and scaling your wealth.

You will be empowered to employ entrepreneurship as a conduit toward achieving your own definition of success and toward building wealth. Enjoy the journey! Enjoy the grind!

For more information or to connect with the author, visit gregbott.com.

Business Acquisition as a Conduit to Wealth

Income can be earned in two overarching ways: through time (hours worked during employment) or capital investment (e.g. stocks, real estate, or business ownership). Although many people can and do become (partially) wealthy off their employment income, there is a limit to that wealth.

There are only so many hours an individual can work over the course of their career, and those are most typically defined by the 40-hour workweek. Sure, you can work harder and increase the number of hours worked, or work smarter and obtain promotions, but there is still a cap on the time available to work in any given week.

As proclaimed by George Clason, author of *The Richest Man in Babylon*, in 1926, "The gold we may retain from our earnings is but the start. The earnings it will make shall build our fortune" (2019, 41). That is, your earnings from investments are not restricted to how many hours you are able to labour in a given period of time. Investments provide the opportunity to make additional money while you are sleeping, and that additional money can make you even more money.

For both the wage-earner and the self-employed, there are numerous instruments available with the goal of increased wealth: savings, guaranteed investment certificates, stocks, mutual funds, index funds, and commercial and residential real estate among others. However, in times of low interest rates on savings, uncertainties and fluctuations in stock markets, global trade disputes, etc., the everyday investor is rightfully frustrated with the options available.

News headlines and economists are constantly claiming to be able to predict the market, telling you when to buy and when to sell. But such headlines often conflict and are thus confusing. There are way too many unexpected variables that affect a global economy to render such predictions accurate. While such analysis provides general context and should not be written off altogether, I wouldn't bet my fortune on such headlines.

Entrepreneurship isn't about being in and out of the market. Rather, it is about recognizing that sometimes there will be headwinds and sometimes there will be tailwinds. It is about having the perseverance to push through the former and to systematically prepare to capitalize on the latter.

Stock markets feel like black boxes to the everyday investor. The challenges of picking individual stock winners and losers are evidenced by the increased popularity of index funds (a portfolio of stocks designed to mimic the market).

The instrument holder has little to no control over these investments. You can educate yourself, read financial reports, and speak with advisers, but then your only input is to hope for the best. It is hard to double the stock of Home Depot or Mastercard, but with business ownership, it is possible to achieve exponential growth. With business ownership, you control the decisions. Every effort that you put in has the potential to provide exponential rewards. Every decision that you make has an impact on your wealth—for better or for worse. You are in the driver's seat.

Entrepreneurs have found a way to remove the cap on potential earnings. It is therefore not surprising that Thomas Stanley and William Danko, authors of *The Millionaire Next Door*, found that "self-employed people make up less than 20 percent of the workers in America but account for two-thirds of the millionaires" (1996, 8). Business ownership can be your conduit to achieving wealth.

Business ownership also has the potential for higher returns in comparison to other instruments. Small businesses trade at a lower price-per-earnings ratio—you get more bang for your buck. This better return is due to a (perceived) high risk versus reward and a lower liquidity (liquidity being the ability to convert an investment into cash). If you are unhappy with your Amazon stock, you sell it. If you are unhappy with your business, well, that problem does not go away with a click of the sell button.

A common perception among the general population is that business ownership is a risky endeavour. A fixation on the start-up has contributed to the perceived risk of business ownership, as start-ups are by their very nature risky. This perception has led many to discount entrepreneurship as an option for themselves, lessening their enthusiasm for including business ownership in their portfolio and their life's journey.

I have also found that business ownership is correlated to wealth for a further reason—because it changes your relationship with money. People often confuse income with wealth. Income is what you earn over the course of a certain time frame, such as a calendar year. It is the number stated on your paycheque. Many people earn a high income from their labour but fail to ever become wealthy. These people have a spending problem. They spend what they earn. As they make more, they spend more.

But for entrepreneurs, wealth is front and center. It is where they place their energy, whether directly or indirectly, every day. When you are responsible for operating a business—revenue generation, rent payments, disbursements to vendors, payroll expense—over time you start to view your personal finances in a new light. You become more alert to the flow of your personal finances and become more reflective on your personal relationship with money. Being forced to increase diligence on business finances spills over into an increased awareness of your personal finances.

Many people associate employment with higher income security. They feel that business ownership is too risky for them. But, as famous financial author Robert Allen rightfully noted in *Multiple Streams of Income*, "Working for someone else, unless you own a piece of the profits, is not security. It is the *illusion* of security" (2000, 34). With a business you will (or should) have hundreds of customers, each one being a source of income. A job is only one source of income. Which do you think is riskier from a revenue perspective?

With business ownership, you have direct control. You have the ability to continually improve your financial knowledge to make decisions that are directly in line with your objectives. You can seek earnings beyond your wage, resume annual earnings beyond your personal exit from daily operations, and have further cash proceeds if you choose to sell the business at some point in the future.

Business ownership is, therefore, a conduit to wealth. But not all approaches to business ownership are created equal. And not all businesses provide the same opportunity for wealth creation and retention. In later sections, I provide a comparison between starting a business and buying an established business. Such an analysis highlights the many benefits of business acquisitions and its favourable attributes in facilitating wealth creation and wealth retention. But a brief introduction is warranted here.

Start-ups often do not provide a palatable risk-reward trade-off, leading to their high failure rate. A start-up can be likened to gambling, and gambling is not the same as investing. Great investors focus on incremental gains, protect themselves from losses, and focus on wealth retention parallel to wealth creation. We are all familiar with Warren Buffett's two rules of investing: rule number one—never lose money, and rule number two—never forget rule number one.

Start-ups may take two, three, four, five, or 10 years before they begin to see any real money coming in, if at all. On the journey to wealth creation, the acquisition accelerates your journey by five or 10 years. And time is an important factor in compounding wealth.

When buying a business, you must think like both an entrepreneur and an investor. This means that you are looking for businesses that have consistent and quantifiable cash flow, which tends to be unpredictable with a start-up.

When buying an existing business, you are buying: a reoccurring revenue stream with a proven history; an existing customer base; tested and refined products or services that have proven to provide value to its customer base; a predictable cash flow stream; a complete team, including a leadership team and a staff base that understands the operations and is able to maintain customer relationships; and existing systems, such as ordering, inventory, operations, and accounting.

Such benefits remove a number of risks that are ever present with a start-up, leapfrogging an entrepreneur's journey toward wealth creation.

BLOOD, SWEAT, AND FEARS

An Authentic Dialogue with Yourself

Howard Schultz, the former CEO of Starbucks, noted that "the entrepreneurial journey is not for everyone. Yes, the highs are high and the rewards can be thrilling. But the lows can break your heart. Entrepreneurs must love what they do to such a degree that doing it is worth the sacrifice and, at times, pain. But doing anything else, we think, would be unimaginable" (Schultz and Gordon 2011, 9). There has to be a passion not only for your end goal but also an appreciation of the journey.

For the millions of everyday entrepreneurs, there is something more: the thrill of the deal, the fulfillment of a greater purpose, the ability to engage with the community in a meaningful way, and a shot at a level of intergenerational wealth that cannot be achieved by limiting one's salary to the hours worked in an employment tenure.

You must have these conversations with yourself. Only by clearly articulating your purpose will you be able to keep going through the lows. Be clear on your inner desires, your passion, your goals and objectives. *Does entrepreneurship provide a pathway to your personal definition of success? If so, you are in for one heck of a ride.*

Anyone can be an entrepreneur. Entrepreneurship is about aligning a business with your core purpose and having a character of perseverance. The rest can be learned. There is nothing that an entrepreneur does that cannot be learned.

But people often cite factors such as age or lack of education as an excuse to quit before they even start. Or they suggest that the timing is not right. There are those who are business owners and those who continually talk about wanting to become business owners but never will.

Corporate ownership is blind to education, to current economic status, and to the number on your birth certificate. Every entrepreneur was once new to entrepreneurship.

Harv Eker wrote a book titled *Secrets of the Millionaire Mind*, explaining the mindset of the rich. Referring to the fact that everyone has to start somewhere, Eker famously proclaimed: "Every master was once a disaster" (2005, 182). His contention is that "it doesn't matter where you are starting from. What matters is that you are willing to learn" because "success is a learnable skill" (Eker 2005, 82).

Education Is Not a Prerequisite

Education is not a prerequisite to entrepreneurship.

I grew up in a small rural community where the largest employers were sizable oil field services and road construction companies. As a kid, I admired the achievements of the owners: the massive amount of equipment that they owned, the number of people they employed, and the size of their contracts.

Looking back, some of these owners had dropped out of high school, while some had passed high school and pursued a trade. Not one had gone to university, and not one had attended business school. Yet they owned some of the most successful companies in the area.

The same is true for many iconic business leaders; the list of those who dropped out of high school or college is a very long list. And a disproportionate number of business leaders have learning disabilities such as dyslexia.

Theo Paphitis is a British entrepreneur and multimillionaire whose holdings have included Ryman and La Senza. In his biography, *Enter the Dragon*, he speaks about the challenges that dyslexia caused in applying for jobs in his younger days, noting that "dyslexia made even the simple act of filling in an application form a major problem" (Paphitis and Stone 2009, 31). Yet he went on to become a multimillionaire through acquiring and turning around failing retailers.

Entrepreneur Jacob Scott[1] also frequently shares about his journey with dyslexia and the fact that he still struggles with reading. Yet Jacob's determination has provided him with multiple millions in real estate holdings and success in business acquisition. In a speech to a fourth-year undergraduate class that I teach, he shared the story of how such a hurdle ultimately became one of the motivating factors of his success.

He noted, "You always had that class where the teacher goes around and everyone reads a few sentences. That was hard for me because people would laugh. And it was hard to deal with at the time. And one day the teacher said that we had to do a class presentation."

He was so afraid to read off the paper that he studied his five-minute speech for over 50 hours. After the grades were counted, the teacher acknowledged it as the best speech in his class. But if the other students averaged 30 minutes to prepare their speeches, he spent 100 times more time preparing for it.

He noted, "And that is what led to my success. That moment for me in elementary was critical, because it showed me the link

---

1 The name of this presenter has been anonymized in the book.

between hard work and outcome. It showed if I worked hard at something, and I outworked everybody, I would have a better outcome than other people."

Dyslexia did not slow down his learning journey. At the same time that he was working at a fast-food restaurant, he read hundreds of books written by or about those who had done what he wanted to accomplish in business, most specifically anything written by Warren Buffett that he could get his hands on.

Jacob has gone on to own over $50 million in real estate and businesses with over $80 million in gross revenue.

His operating philosophy is to purchase businesses that have operated for at least 20 years and have a minimum of 50 employees—businesses that he feels he can help grow over the next 10 years.

Sound familiar to the philosophies regarding business acquisitions presented in this book?

Stanford professors Jeffery Pfeffer and Robert Sutton similarly note in *The Knowing-Doing Gap* that "numerous researchers have found that little of what is taught in college or even business schools really prepares would-be managers for the realities of managing" (2000, 3). I would suggest that this finding is amplified for the complexities of entrepreneurship.

In fact, education can often be a hurdle. It can pigeonhole your thoughts and obstruct your creativity. Formal education trains you to be a good employee, to think inside the box, and to comply with the norms of business. Even business schools and MBA programs prepare you to get a "better job" and to move up the ranks of employment by becoming more valuable to your employer.

Thomas Stanley spent most of his career researching the affluent. In a study of millionaires, Stanley (2001) found that most have been told at some point in their lives—by an authority figure or by the results of a standardized test score—that they are not intellectually gifted or smart enough to succeed.

Although most of the millionaires surveyed believed that they had benefited from their education, they indicated that their school or college experience was "influential in determining that hard work was more important than genetic high intellect in achieving" (Stanley 2001, 15). Under such a presupposition, it could be further argued that, at some point, further education in preparation for your journey is doing nothing more than delaying your journey.

In economics, there's a term called diminishing marginal returns, which simply means that although adding more of something may still add value, that additional value becomes less over time. Applying this theory to education suggests that early programs provide a foundation or base, but any additional education beyond such a base adds less value to your knowledge and corresponding opportunities than the previous program.

What is more important than formal education is the willingness to learn and to learn from your experiences as you go through your personal journey of entrepreneurship. Great entrepreneurs develop the gift of applying and following through on knowledge.

Management writer Peter Drucker has been quoted as noting that the "only skill that will be important in the 21st century is the skill of learning new skills. Everything else will become obsolete over time" (quoted in Tracy 2017, 96). Stanley and Danko rightfully note: "Remember, wealth is blind. It cares not if its patrons are well educated" (1996, 75). All this is not to suggest that education holds no value to entrepreneurship. It is to suggest that it is not a strict prerequisite.

There Will Never Be a Good Time to Start

The same can be said for experience. The only way to learn how to start and run a company is to start and run a company—and by reading my book, of course!

Although there may be certain disciplines that can be learned from textbooks or from formal settings—such as accounting, finance, engineering, sales, and marketing—that will help you to perform select functions within a business, to truly understand what it is like to be in the trenches of operating a business, to have a team's future relying on your every decision, and to juggle multiple roles at once can only be studied and mastered through practice.

All entrepreneurs were once not entrepreneurs. They come from all walks of life, different educational backgrounds, ages, and experiences. As legendary development writer Brian Tracy noted in *Millionaire Dollar Habits*, "You can write the script of your own life, and if you are not happy with the current script, you can rip it up and write a new one" (Tracy 2017, xvii).

This does not mean that you should not prepare. What it does mean is that lack of experience is no excuse. Seek advice from those who are achieving what you wish to achieve. Pick up a book, or 50 books, or learn from other successful entrepreneurs on YouTube or podcasts. You will never feel completely prepared, so if you wait for that special feeling, you will never embark on any journey.

In a speech to a fourth-year undergraduate class that I teach, Jacob Scott explained that "you have to start before you are ready, because you are never going to be ready. If you wait until you are ready, it is never going to happen, and you are going to lose the opportunity."

You have the choice to "eke out the last ten, twenty, thirty years of your life in a state of preservation rather than growth," or you can start "experiencing the high that comes from putting yourself out there and trying something new" (Dickinson 2019, 35).

Find Your Strength at Any Age

Arianna Huffington started her first company, *The Huffington Post*, in 2005 and shortly after was recognized as one of *Time* magazine's Most Influential People (Huffington 2014). She was 55 years of age at the time. She later sold *The Huffington Post* for $315 million and went on to other great achievements.

The media's focus on high-tech companies has led to an inordinate amount of attention being given to young individuals who have invented something new or developed a new way of doing something. As the story goes, young, youthful … billionaire by a young age.

However, this narrative is not the reality for most entrepreneurs; it provides a false perception that entrepreneurship is reserved for young people who jump in, risking it all, without any value given to experience, mentorship, or proper planning. A behaviour of taking excessive risks is held up as a required attribute.

This account further dissuades those observers who form the view that this is what an entrepreneur is supposed to look like. They cannot look in the mirror and see themselves as conforming to this stereotype. They thus convince themselves that they do not look like what an entrepreneur is supposed to look like.

However, life experience and age do matter. As with employment, relationships, and performing surgery, experience matters. With it comes years of enhancement to one's management skills and increased wisdom in decision-making. There are strengths within each age bracket—find yours and embrace it. Focus on your strength and build your team with people who compensate for your blind spots.

A study of US data found the average age of an entrepreneur to be 42 when they started their company and the average age of a successful start-up founder—success determined by highest growth—to be 45 (Azoulay et al. 2018). Their study in the *Harvard Business Review* suggests that success in entrepreneurship increases with age, which they credit, in part, to work experience.

In *Burn the Business Plan*, a book aimed largely at revealing the fact that most popular ideas about entrepreneurship are wrong,

Carl Schramm, a professor at Syracuse University finds "the average entrepreneur is nearly forty years old when he launches, and more than eighty percent of all new companies are started by people over thirty-five" (2018, 2).

He then goes on to conclude that "more entrepreneurs are between forty-five and fifty-five than any other cohort, and entrepreneurs over fifty-five create more companies than those under thirty-five. And—another surprise—the chances of a new company surviving rises with the age of the entrepreneur" (Schramm 2018, 2).

Angela Duckworth has found that as individuals age, they mature and increase in their grit. As she notes in her book, *Grit*, an individual's passion for their work "is a little bit of discovery, followed by a lot of development, and then a lifetime of deepening" (2016, 103). It takes time to find your stride and to develop your purpose. But you are more likely to find it by being engaged in and intentional about your journey than you would by sitting on the sidelines.

As I contended earlier, successful entrepreneurs are those who have found their passion and purpose. If you cannot stick to it, entrepreneurship is not something that you will be successful at. It is a long-term game, a lifetime journey.

The average age of a successful entrepreneur is not the 20-year-old who developed a revolutionary software in their parents' basement. It is more likely to be someone in their second or third career who has experiences upon which to build.

You Do Not Need Money to Make Money

There is also an odd misconception among aspiring business own-ers that you need to be wealthy in order to start on your entre-preneurial journey and that you require massive wealth to start or to purchase a company. I understand how this belief is formed in one's mind, but think about it for a minute: is an athlete in peak shape before they train or an artist skillful before finding their passion?

If you feel that you are not able to start on your entrepreneurial journey because the health of your current finances is an unsurmountable hurdle, then you are simply not thinking creatively enough. I develop this thought further in subsequent sections on partnerships and financing, but the short version is that you must be able to articulate the value that you bring to a business and to a partnership. Money will follow those who bring energy and knowledge into the room.

In my first business, I brought the youthful energy, the sleepless nights, the grit, and the ability to put together an ownership and investment team. That was my contribution and my value to the group. There will always be others who have capital but who do not want to take on the role of managing partner. They will need you as much as you need them. You simply need to demonstrate the value that you are able to bring. As I continue to develop as an entrepreneur and as a person, I am exposed to further experiences, and where I am able to provide value has shifted. Find your worth, your value, your legitimacy.

In an examination of multiple case studies of individuals who had successfully acquired sizable businesses, Harvard professors Ruback and Yudkoff concluded that "none had bought a business before or had significant wealth when they started, and all of them raised money from investors to complete their acquisition" (2017, 5).

Do not let false perceptions hold you back from achieving your own success.

I can guarantee that, at some point, you will have setbacks and will lose money—whereas those on the sidelines may not. But I can even more certainly guarantee that you will not make money in business if you are not in business; fear of losing paralyzes most people—both in business and in life.

If you are able to articulate your passions and your purpose, and you feel that entrepreneurship can be a conduit to success, do not let any fears and false perceptions (excuses) hold you back. I still have countless setbacks ahead of me, but I want to be able to look back and say that I gave this thing that we call life an honest try. "Some people accomplish an extraordinary amount with their lives, as opposed to the great majority who accomplish very little. These peak performers or self-actualizers seem to earn more money; have better families, friends, and relationships; enjoy higher levels of health and energy; achieve much higher levels of success, esteem, and prestige in their fields; and live longer, happier lives than the average" (Tracy 2017, 151–152). Which of these people would you rather be?

Are You Actually an Entrepreneur?

Although what entrepreneurs do can be defined, it is impossible to define who entrepreneurs are. Their backgrounds, experiences, education, ages, and personalities vary widely. While some are focused and analytical, others are quirky and eccentric. While some are extroverts who command a room, others are introverts and apply such experiences and qualities to their success.

Prior to writing this section, I reflected on my own experiences and on the qualities of successful entrepreneurs that I know. I then read widely, including business books and numerous biographies and autobiographies of successful entrepreneurs. Based on all of this, I have come to one conclusion: entrepreneurs exhibit perseverance—also commonly referred to as grit, determination, or stick-with-it-ness. It is that simple.

Sure, there are other skills, experiences, and attributes that help entrepreneurs with daily operations—many of which I will briefly outline—but it is perseverance that keeps them pushing through the hard times.

A typical examination of preparing for entrepreneurship lists skills such as accounting, payroll, human resources, time management, client relations, operations, and systems. These are important, but they can easily be learned, and in most cases, delegated or outsourced. Entrepreneurial success is less about hard skills and more about character—attributes of self-awareness, acceptance of failure, work ethic, a willingness to embrace uncertainty and chaos, and, ultimately, perseverance.

Entrepreneurs Are Self-Aware

The requirement of being self-aware as a success factor of entrepreneurship enters at many stages of the journey. Self-awareness is first required when reflecting on your personal capacity, strengths, and weaknesses in determining whether this journey is right for you. Compiling a personal inventory of such qualities will quickly help you to examine—through self-awareness—whether you should be an entrepreneur.

Once you are certain of your journey, and have taken inventory of your strengths and weaknesses, self-awareness further contributes to your success at two other points of reflection. Often completed in parallel, these include addressing and improving your weaknesses (aka temporary limitations) and surrounding yourself with people who compensate for them.

A critical fork in the road to success is an entrepreneur's ability to put together a team that offsets their personal capabilities. Whether I am setting up a start-up or an acquisition transition team or managing the day-to-day grind, my first order of business involves reflecting on my strengths and weaknesses and putting in place individuals who are able to fill in my skill and personality gaps.

During my tenure of owning and operating restaurants, I periodically found myself as an interim general manager. Recognizing my strengths in analytics and systems, but not being overly inspirational, my first order of business was to identify high-energy leaders who had a natural ability to rally the troops. Often, these individuals were not overly organized—the types that tend to show up late because they cannot find their keys—and were not strong at identifying business trends and thus reacting to the needs of the business. That was okay because those were things that I could do. What I needed was someone who could inspire, someone with a presence that people wanted to be around.

Entrepreneur, innovator, and billionaire Jack Ma eagerly admits, "I am not the most talented person. My appearance, abilities, and education are far from society's best" (Lee and Song 2016, 55). Yet, his journey to success is among the most interesting and inspiring business cases. After being introduced to the internet while on a trip to the US in 1995, he decided to bring the internet to China (Lee and Song 2016). Ma has since led his company Alibaba to become one of the world's largest e-commerce companies. Originally an English school teacher, Ma himself has achieved a net worth of over $47 billion according to Forbes ("Jack Ma" n.d.).

Know what you are good at and what you are not. Know what your personal strategic advantage is. Without this knowledge—obtained through honest reflection—you will come up against others out there, competing against you, who are clear on their professional strategic advantage. And that is a dangerous space to be in.

Before moving forward, reflect on the following questions for a minute:

- What are your personal strengths that provide a professional strategic advantage?
- What do you enjoy learning about? What do you not enjoy learning about?
- What are the relevant gaps in your personal abilities that could hinder your success in operating a great company?

- Which gaps are so fundamental to your success that you must work toward self-improvement? Which of these gaps are easily outsourced?

Acceptance of Failure

Although they may feel gut wrenching when they happen, setbacks and failures are our best teachers. I would be more inclined to invest in an entrepreneur who has made mistakes and has learned from them than in one who has yet to be educated by the school of hard knocks. Any setback is about the experience gained and about reflection and learning.

At one point in my journey, my investment group had ownership across multiple restaurants. At one particular site where we owned a minority stake, our managing partner—a company that was a large player in this space—assumed the responsibility of operating it. The site struggled with sales and operations for several years, until one day when we drove by and saw that the doors had been closed. Our half a million dollars disappeared along with it.

Although the financial loss was significant to my net worth, it was the embarrassment and the hit to my ego that took the biggest toll. We had a strong reputation in the industry as being a successful operator and of being an employer of choice. I silently grumbled in my own head, having continual conversations with myself for a number of years, placing blame on everyone but my wonderful self.

Then one day I realized that I had contributed to the loss. I chose to invest in the venture and had chosen to move forward despite not having majority control. With this realization, I could then trace my steps back to the initial investment decisions and finally see the series of decisions that contributed to the loss of the investment. Our cash injection was no more than playing the stock market. We were not investing—we were gambling. And even worse, we were gambling without liquidity. Without an exit strategy.

Once I realized this, I was able to take ownership in my own mind. And with that, I could mentally log personal investment principles to inform the 2-point-0 of my journey. From this one example, I was able to formulate a series of investment principles that would inform my future decision-making.

Only once I was able to accept this was I able to move forward with a deeper sense of reflection and discovery and move forward with a more methodical and principle-based approach toward investing. This includes, for example, having majority control, having clear partnership agreements that provide for eventual exits from the partnership, and ensuring that everyone agrees to continual structured communication.

More often than not, the fear of failure is not about the failure itself, but a fear of the vulnerability of putting yourself out there and of the embarrassment of failing publicly.

My second realization from this experience was that nobody looked at me differently; the embarrassment was only a product of self-infliction. *If you maintain integrity and are honest in your dealings, then failures are nothing more than the tuition of life's education.*

This one lesson also further allowed for broader reflection and a realization that I have held myself back from other prospects that were well calculated to be opportunities because the perceived risk of personal loss (or ego) was more prominent than the risk of financial loss.

In *Think and Grow Rich*, Napoleon Hill provided valuable insight in proclaiming that "failure is a trickster with a keen sense of irony and cunning. It takes great delight in tripping one when success is almost in reach" (1960, 5). Successful entrepreneurs— the ones who endure, decade after decade—experience failure time and time again yet continue to persevere. It isn't about whether you will experience setbacks but about how you bounce back.

Successful entrepreneur and *Dragon's Den* personality Arlene Dickinson has noted that "every successful entrepreneur I know has experienced her share of failures: near bankruptcies, product recalls, inability to secure adequate financing, or just a good old-fashioned lack of customers" (2013, 215).

Her *Dragon's Den* colleague Kevin O'Leary has similarly noted, "I've made mistakes, inched close to bankruptcy, been sued, fired, and slandered. I've despaired about making payroll and have taken some detours that were ill advised" (2011, 5). O'Leary started his career by building a software company and currently invests across multiple companies.

Looking through a bit more optimistic lens, Jason Fried and David Hansson have suggested that failure is not a prerequisite for success and that one should not be fooled by the statistics: "Other people's failures are just that: *other* people's failures" (Fried and Hansson 2010, 16).

Sure, diligent planning can help you avoid large-scale failures—and I do not contend that near bankruptcies are inevitable—but mistakes will be made, and "very few businesspeople hit a home run in their first time at bat" (Herjavec and Reynolds 2010, 40).

Felix Dennis similarly articulates that "the biggest basket I ever built wasn't my first or second. It was my twentieth. But if I hadn't built the second, I would never have reached the twentieth. And maybe, just maybe, I have a couple more baskets yet to build" (Dennis 2006, 128). Dennis is a British multimillionaire who built his fortune in the publishing industry. His story is one about reflecting on your failures and building your next venture upon the lessons learned. This is very true for most successful business owners—their first business is rarely their forever business.

As I continue to build personal capacity along my own entrepreneurial journey, I continue to develop principles for both my business and personal realms. These principles are not entirely static; they are constantly refined as I learn and continue my personal development. If something did not go as planned, an honest self-reflection and a situational post-mortem helps to bring clarity as to why it did not work. I then document what I will do differently the next time that I am presented with a similar situation.

Work Ethic of the Wealthy

Entrepreneurs work hard. This point is self-explanatory but often forgotten and significantly underestimated. There is a common perception that, if you own the place, you can do as you please and set your own schedule—after all, you are the boss.

Although there are business authors who claim to have figured out how to use business as a conduit to a work-life balance—Timothy Ferriss's *The 4-Hour Work Week* (2007), and Courtney and Carter Reum's *Shortcut Your Startup* (2018)—this is not the consensus among successful entrepreneurs.

My personal experience is that—at least in the early stages—most entrepreneurs struggle to find a work-life balance. In the first number of years in business, it is not uncommon to work months on end without a complete day off. Two years into our current company, my business partner unsuccessfully attempted a five-day holiday but was quickly reminded that, as a business owner, your customers own you. Your staff own you.

Elon Musk provides the same repetitive response in interviews when asked about his success, claiming to continually work 80 to 100 hours a week; a factor that he claims singularly provides him a chance of two and a half times the level of productivity of someone working a typical 40-hour work week.

In subsequent chapters, I advise wannabe entrepreneurs to aim for sizable companies or to scale small companies into larger ones. Organizations require a certain level of revenue and cash flow in order to be able to delegate to professional management. Your goal should be to get out of the trenches. There is always someone out there with better management skills than you. Hire that person and let them operate the day-to-day.

Once your business has been scaled to a level where this is possible, you are able to step out of the trenches. Although you can never be completely removed, what you do shifts. At that point, your personal involvement and hours worked become a personal decision. This is also the point at which you can go out and buy more companies if you so desire!

But most successful entrepreneurs never slow down; work ethic is in their blood. Jack Ma has said it best: "I once thought when your company starts to grow the boss can relax a little. Instead, I'm more tired than ever! An entrepreneur constantly confronts crises—a good thing. Better to deal daily with small pains inside the company before they turn into a cancer" (Lee and Song 2016, 46).

Billionaire investor and author Ray Dalio similarly noted, "It's obvious to me now that while one gets better at things over time, it doesn't become any easier if one is also progressing to higher levels—the Olympic athlete finds his sport to be every bit as challenging as the novice does" (2017, 71). Very true.

Embrace Uncertainty and Chaos

Entrepreneurs also build up resilience through being overwhelmed with chaos. In the early stages of my entrepreneurial journey, I would become quite flustered with the chaos and corresponding busyness.

This attribute of entrepreneurs has not always received the attention it deserves. However, in recognizing the importance of embracing chaos, business journalist Amanda Lang authored a book titled *The Beauty of Discomfort*. After examining how successful people become and stay successful, her main thesis was that "truly successful people don't merely tolerate discomfort—

they embrace it, seeking it out again and again. And their comfort with discomfort is what makes them so good at change. They seem to experience discomfort as a positive rather than a negative force, and they find a way to use it to motive themselves to achieve" (Lang 2017, 8).

Elon Musk often talks about a business owner's time being spent on all of the things that are going wrong within the company, as there is no point in spending time on the things that are going right.

An entrepreneur must continually navigate such uncertainty, be aware of the internal and external environment, and make decisions with incomplete information. Chaos and uncertainty can paralyze business school–trained managers yet invigorate entrepreneurs.

This does not mean that you should not aim to control chaos, *as it is only with systems and processes—turning chaos into routine— that you are able to scale a business.* What it does mean is that you should not panic in the chaos: successful entrepreneurs, the ones who make it big and give it all that they have got, move into uncharted territory, whether it be a new venture or product line or an acquisition, by embracing change.

Perseverance, Resilience, and Grit

One of the most interesting company narratives in the world is the Tata Group, now operating in over 100 countries. It is said that the company's founder, Jamsetji Tata, travelled across India for 17 years in search of an iron ore deposit of sufficient quality to set up an iron and steel manufacturing plant (Kuber 2019). The Tata Group (Tata Steel) is now a major player in the world steel market.

If there is one universal truth about the spirit of entrepreneurs, it is that they display perseverance, also broadly referred to as grit, resilience, determination, or stick-with-it-ness. This comes in two forms: staying with something for the long haul and staying on task despite setbacks.

Entrepreneurship is not a sprint, but a marathon. Studies have shown that it takes somewhere in the neighbourhood of five to 10 years to become a master at a certain skill. But entrepreneurship has complexities and takes place within an ever-evolving external environment—e.g. shifting customer expectations, technological advances, societal trends, and staff expectations. It is safe to say that it is not a short-term play.

In her book titled *Grit*, Angela Duckworth found that "grit is more about stamina than intensity" (2016, 53) and that gritty people do not skip around from one pursuit to another. Rather, grit "is about working on something you care about so much that you're willing to stay loyal to it" (Duckworth 2016, 54).

It is also easier to persevere when you have found something that you are passionate about.

We have already discussed those who just talk about entrepreneurship and those who follow through. The former are defeated even before they start, as the number of times they try, fall, and get back up is zero. "The majority of people are ready to throw their aims and purposes overboard, and give up at the first sign of opposition or misfortune. A few carry on despite all opposition, until they attain their goal" (Hill 1960, 131). But, to stick with it, you need to have clearly articulated your goals and passions.

This isn't to suggest that perseverance is reserved exclusively for entrepreneurs. Athletes, cancer patients, farmers, parents, and many others display these traits every day. Perseverance is prevalent within many people, professions, and activities. But it is clear that successful entrepreneurs, those who stick it out and eventually succeed, demonstrate attributes of grit, resilience, determination, and stick-with-it-ness.

Preparing for Your Journey

Is It Possible to Be a Part-Time Entrepreneur?

Partial focus only builds partial businesses. Would you enter a marriage with a part-time effort, or would you give it your full attention? If you enter it on a casual basis, you will quickly find yourself kicked to the curb.

It is quite common to hear people say that they are entering entrepreneurship on a part-time basis. They want to maintain their employment income and have a safety net in case the business does not work out. "Because of the high likelihood of failure, as many as seventy percent of all new entrepreneurs attempt to mitigate the risk of starting a new business by continuing to hold down a full-time job. Being a part-time entrepreneur, however, is highly correlated to a lower probability of success" (Schramm 2018, 237).

Entrepreneurship is a unique beast. It is a personal and professional journey, a lifestyle. In the early years, it will take all that you have. As Arlene Dickinson rightfully notes, "You can't sign up for the entrepreneurial life with a part-time commitment. The nature of the game is that success as an entrepreneur will take everything you have and then some. You have to be all in" (2013, 209).

If you do plan to start part-time—perhaps in the planning or search stage—I suggest that you be clear in your own mind as to when you plan to quit your employment. Perhaps it is based on a timeline, such as three months before launch, or on a milestone, such as when you hit 10 customers.

You might chug along fine for a while, but without a full-time commitment it will not scale, and it will not build wealth. Some academics go as far as to recommend that those who are serious about the journey quit their jobs during the search stage (e.g. see Ruback and Yudkoff 2017). I understand that this is scary to hear, but if you do not burn your ships behind you, retreat is inevitable.

We all know the saying that if you have more than a couple of priorities, you have no priorities at all. If your employment continues to dictate your schedule, consume your energy, and retain ownership of your capacity for creative space, your business will not receive the attention required to reach its potential.

For some, their bright ideas occur during a walk or their morning shower. I often wake up to a number of emails from myself, sent between midnight and two a.m. when my brain is churning. When my mind is consumed with multiple projects, each project is competing for the midnight creative juices. But when my mind is singularly focused, all cylinders are working toward the singular goal.

There are exceptions to this. If you want to have a side hustle or a part-time gig, if your objective is to stay small and earn money on the side, then that is fine. But that is not what this book is about. This book is about taking ownership of your life and using business ownership as a conduit to being financially whole and complete. For that, it is a full-time commitment and mindset.

Pre-entrepreneurship

Although anyone can be an entrepreneur—regardless of age, education, current financial standing, or any other excuse that you can muster—this does not mean that you shouldn't prepare. Although preparation can look quite different for each person, the path I would suggest for those in employment is to plan your pre-entrepreneurial career around accumulating the most relevant experiences. Learn multiple skills and move between departments. Place yourself in leadership and decision-making roles.

Some entrepreneurs take this one step further, noting that "you should have no long-term, or even medium-term, requirements of the first two or three companies you work for. Promotion is always welcome and brings with it the opportunity to learn more, but you are there to ensure that you take every opportunity to suck the marrow of what you need to know, to understand it and place it within a greater context for future purpose. The purpose of getting rich" (Dennis 2006, 44).

My early career involved finance and accounting roles within a large organization. I had great mentors and the company provided me with many opportunities to move around and to take on different roles. I still lean on these experiences for functions such as budgeting, accounting, benchmarking, and creating dashboards.

But I was so junior in my career that I missed out on the opportunity of managing people. At the time, I knew that I was restless for something more, but when I took a leave of absence to take my first master's program, I did not know that I would never work for someone else again (aside from instructing at the university, but that is self-development and a purposeful hobby). When I jumped into entrepreneurship, I immediately had a staff of about 35 and had never had anyone report to me before. Did I learn quickly? Sure. But a more purposeful experience prior to turning to entrepreneurship would have helped with this skillset.

For those of you in your early careers, aspiring to be entrepreneurs, I make the suggestion to be very purposeful in your preparation. Work for organizations that can provide you with a breadth of skills and knowledge. Ask to transfer between multiple departments so that you are exposed to a variety of experiences, such as operations, accounting, and human resources. Seek out mentors and supervisors who have the ability and willingness to make an impact on your development.

Read about topics in your current and intended fields. Listen to podcasts, network, observe, and be a sponge for knowledge. As Brian Tracy pointed out, "an average person who develops the habit of lifelong learning will eventually run circles around a genius who goes home and watches television each night" (2017, 59). Get in the habit of reading, thinking, and applying what you learn. *It's not about formal education; it's about your capacity and willingness to apply knowledge and about following through, persistently, over the long-term.*

I find that most employees are too fixated on their immediate pay, as opposed to taking a long-term view. If you are reading this book and are currently in employment, I encourage you to focus on gaining experience and exposure to diverse opportunities. Focus less on what each opportunity pays and more on how such experiences can prepare you for what is to come.

Focus on developing your greatest asset—your mind. That will serve you for many years. Money will follow. But often, with entry-level jobs, there is a negative correlation between compensation and opportunity; the jobs that pay the most right out of school are unlikely to be the same roles that will prepare you for a long-term career progression or entrepreneurship.

Within the restaurant industry, we had countless examples of servers who made big money—and the more they made, the fancier their cars were—passing up management opportunities because the advancement did not come with the big cash tips. Those who were willing to forego short-term earnings and rotate through management positions often found the benefits of such mindsets quite soon as they moved up the organizational chart. Many developed their skills and were rewarded when they had developed their capacity to move on to their own ventures.

Once you get a taste of a routine paycheque it becomes a comfort. Both Robert Kiyosaki (author of *Rich Dad Poor Dad*) and Kevin O'Leary often speak of employment and the paycheque as a drug. It usually goes something like this: salary is the drug they give you to help you forget about your dreams, and it is a hard cycle to break. If you are currently not living out your dream, does this resonate with you?

Life rewards those who are prepared. Entrepreneurship is no exception to this rule. How do you plan to prepare? Whatever path you choose, be intentional about it, tailor it to your personal end goals, and plan to prepare with a purpose.

Section Summary

Now that we have looked behind the curtain to find who an entre-preneur is, I hope I have not scared you but have motivated you. If you are still reading, you likely have what it takes. The next step, before moving forward in your journey, is to be clear on your per-sonal purpose. What do you seek in life, and is entrepreneurship the right conduit to achieving it?

I ask you to examine your true self and your sincere desires in order to create a personal mission statement. This will help you determine whether entrepreneurship is truly right for you. However, once you pass this hurdle, once you say to yourself that this journey is indeed for you, I say to you that there are no limits to where your entrepreneurial journey can take you—financial freedom and completeness, personal fulfillment, a sense of purpose. If you can dream it, entrepreneurship can be your conduit to achieving it.

If it is strictly wealth that you seek, you will fail. It will be a miserable journey. If it is simply financial freedom, a purposeful career, and time off with a pension that you seek, these things can be achieved through a myriad of other meaningful avenues. To be successful at anything, you must enjoy the journey and not just covet the results. Successful entrepreneurship is an all-in, a life's journey.

STRATEGY OF ACQUIRING SUSTAINABLE WEALTH

Become the Rightful Owner

As you will have discovered by this point, self-awareness and self-discovery are important factors in your journey to success. Although self-discovery is an ever-evolving process of experimentation, before you get started on your journey there are a number of important questions that you must first address:

- What do you require from your relationship with your future company?
- What level of income and what lifestyle do you plan to eventually achieve? (Note that it is *plan* to achieve, not *hope* to achieve.)
- What skillset, abilities, and passions do you have?
- What type of company does your skillset support?
- What role do you want to eventually play within your organization?
- How does your role within the organization relate to your nonbusiness goals within your family and the greater community?

Clear answers to these questions will provide clarity on the profile of the company that you seek. Although this may seem simple on the surface, I have seen really smart people starting or acquiring the wrong businesses. They had great management skills and processes and worked long hours for many years, but their talents were wasted on the barriers and struggles unique to their chosen business or industry. Sometimes it was because they thought too small, but more fundamentally, it was because they had chosen the wrong business. I will help guide you through such consideration.

Start with what you require from a business. Most people do not get into business with the intention of making less money than they would have if they had stayed in employment. However, for the overwhelming majority, this is the case. The vast majority of new business owners work harder than they ever had before and earn much less.

Although lack of preparation, insufficient management skills, or undercapitalization do play a factor, the main reasons are more fundamental but are often overlooked. Common errors include:

- choosing a company based on the (perceived) desirability of the industry, rather than matching one's skillset to a company profile,
- a fixation on the lure of the start-up, overlooking acquisition as an alternative opportunity,
- a lack of predefined principles in place prior to the search process and a lack of purposeful thought into what an enduring company looks like—choosing glamour over substance, or
- an incomplete understanding of the search process and of the depth of search required.

A thoughtful examination of such factors will help you find a business for which you are the "rightful owner." You are the rightful owner of a business when your passion, energy, and abilities are in line with the strategic needs of the organization.

As a general rule, people are commonly attracted to the get-rich-quick perception that attaches itself to glamorous businesses—

hospitality, tech companies, internet companies—which additionally tend to have lower barriers to entry.

When I was in the restaurant business, I was constantly approached by customers—wannapreneurs—asking about starting a restaurant. They would say things like "you guys are always busy; you must make a lot of money," "how much does it cost to open one of these," or "it must be fun owning a restaurant." There is a certain allure to the high energy and the youthful attraction of such businesses. But the reality is that it is a tough and cyclical industry.

This does not mean that you should do something you hate. Of course not. Be quick to rule out sectors that do not resonate with you. If you cannot find passion, you will lose energy quickly. It won't work. But I do suggest that you not narrow your search based on an initial fixation on a select industry.

There tends to be a negative correlation between industries that appear to be glamorous and those that are profitable in the long haul. This observation has also been noted by a number of business authors. Aaron Muller, author of *the Lifestyle Business Owner*, noted that "the more glamorous the business is, the less profitable it tends to be" (Muller 2018, 64).

Stanley and Danko refer to companies that are commonly owned by self-made millionaires and that perform well over time as "dull-normal" (Stanley and Danko 1996, 237). And in their *HBR Guide to Buying a Small Business*, Ruback and Yudkoff similarly noted that "dull" businesses are "terrific business opportunities" (2017, 10), as they are more likely to yield stable incomes over time. And they further stated, "We recommend against buying a tech company or any business in a volatile industry" (Ruback and Yudkoff 2017, 10).

The investment style of Warren Buffett follows a similar trajectory. He was criticized for staying clear of internet stocks while they were fashionable, and they subsequently crashed (Schroeder

2008). And he has refrained from adding any amount of Bitcoin to his holdings. He uses the phrase "durable competitive advantage" when referring to companies that show signs of lasting profitability.

The more durable and stable companies owned by everyday millionaires often fly under the radar of the average person. Many do not have storefronts, so we are not constantly reminded of their existence. The work that they perform goes unnoticed, often after the typical nine-to-fiver heads home to put their feet up after work or after they tuck in for the night.

If you head out for a beer with your friends, the name of the trendy establishment will be front of mind, but do you ever stop to consider whose machines swept the parking lot, how the high windows were cleaned, who leases and services the cooking equipment, how the linens are being magically replenished, or who owns the building?

Successful entrepreneurship "has less to do with what's done in a business and more to do with how it's done. The commodity isn't what's important—the way it's delivered is" (Gerber 1995, 73). "The true product of a business is the business itself" (Gerber 1995, 83). So, do not be fixated on what a business does. Be cognizant on what abilities you have to contribute to an organization.

Skills Are Transferable Across Industries

When looking for their next venture, many aspiring entrepreneurs become fixated on a particular industry or micro sector within it. This may be relevant criterion if you are a dentist, physiotherapist, accountant, dog groomer, or lawyer looking to break out and start your own practice. But, for everyone else, this tends to be an unproductive search limitation and often has unintended consequences.

Skills are transferable. This is evident in the fact that the current working generation often moves between industries multiple times during their working tenure. Rather than being fixated on an industry, it is more productive to take stock of your ambitions, purpose, experiences, and skillset. You can find a calling within almost any business. You can find purpose in helping others, in mentoring, or in whatever else you may fancy.

One of the early reviewers of this book was a friend of mine who demonstrates this point quite well. She was a successful veterinarian who now owns a company in automotive financing and, most recently, owns a business that distributes subscriptions of dog care packages. Her comments were, "I really liked the section on transferrable skills. After finding myself in completely different industries, confidence arose with an understanding of my skills and abilities. I can take that anywhere!"

Seeking a business based on your current industry or trade not only narrows your search, but more importantly, often creates an impediment to success. Having an intimate knowledge of a product or service can create a focus on the wrong priorities. A chef may focus solely on the food, a mechanic may gravitate to the shop floor, or a plumber may want to inspect every toilet installation.

When this happens, business owners can become so immersed in detail that they become blind to the more important strategic priorities. As legendary business author Michael Gerber is often quoted as saying, "Go to work *on* your business rather than *in* it" (1995, 109).

Additionally, the "conditions of industry change so fast that long experience is in some trades almost a disadvantage, and in many it is of far less value than a quickness in taking hold of new ideas and adapting one's habits to new conditions" (Alfred Marshall, quoted in Freeland 2012, 51).

If you are strong on sales, for example, you will want to find a company with strong operations but lacking modern sales techniques. Here, you could have an immediate impact toward adding value and see an almost instant increase in profitability. It matters not what the business sells. The fresh energy that you inject into modernizing the marketing strategies of the organization will prove to increase revenue almost immediately.

If you have a strong track record of managing people in one industry, it will transfer to another. Management is management. You will figure it out. If you are experienced in supply chain management and have a passion for logistical systems, you may gravitate toward distribution. The specific product being distributed is of little importance.

Business owners often burn out, especially if they have fought against the headwinds associated with a start-up. They lose the ability to step into work each day and view things through an objective lens. The great majority of companies that have stood the test of time are therefore operating on outdated systems—outdated sales functions, obsolete inventory management, for example—and have become complacent in regard to customer service.

Find a business for which you are the rightful owner. You are the rightful owner of a business when your passion, energy, and abilities are in line with the strategic needs of the organization. This is where you will find success.

Find a company that has stood the test of time, but one in which the inefficiencies match your passion. The existing cash flow of an enduring company paired with the fresh energy of an aspiring entrepreneur is a dynamite combination.

Acquisitions for Wealth

The Infamous Start-up

The next decision you need to make on your journey is whether to start a company from scratch or to acquire an existing company. This is another area where folklore tends to lead wannapreneurs down a dangerous path. All too often, we hear friends, family, and colleagues talking about wanting to start a business doing such and such. But how often do you hear these same individuals talking about buying an existing business? Rarely, if ever.

Benefits of a start-up are many, including the ability to set up a company with a clean slate. There is value in being able to create a business with no customer preconceptions about your brand or to start with organizational structures and assets that have not simply evolved over time, giving you the opportunity to be quite intentional about them. Or you may have a brilliant mind with an innovative idea that can only go to market though a start-up because no such business currently exists.

I have been involved at the ownership level with numerous start-ups and acquisitions. From these experiences, and from researching widely on the experiences of others, I have—as you will have observed—a strong bias toward acquiring an existing company when focused on a journey of wealth creation.

Our minds have been trained to think about entrepreneurship and the start-up as synonyms. The story of the start-up is a sexy story: the youthful coder working in their parents' basement and turning it into a billion-dollar global empire or the determined distributor initially selling out of their parents' garage before they make it big on the international stage.

Start-up groups have formed in most major cities across North America, providing networking, mentoring, and peer support. Such organizations have done a great job building a social media presence and following. Television programs such as *Dragon's Den* and *Shark Tank* have also contributed to the perceived fame and glory associated with the start-up.

The issue with start-ups is that they do not provide a palatable risk-reward trade-off, leading to their high failure rate. With a start-up, it is more "likely that you end up getting less money than you would in a salaried position and yet, you spend more time at the office than at home. And there's the real prospect that the business you've spent money, time and energy nurturing from inception won't last more than five years" (Jay 2019, 11).

But their allure keeps sucking people in. And I have to admit that I have fallen for their pull and will likely do so again. Will I have the willpower and self-discipline to follow my own business principles? There is a certain unexplainable thrill in starting a company. But the same can probably be said for cocaine.

However, the thrill tends not to have the same financial rewards when compared to buying an established company. Through a truly objective lens, the financial return on investment, especially when placing a value on your time, is not conducive to a start-up. The math just doesn't add up.

This is probably a good time to revisit Warren Buffett's two rules of investing: rule number one—never lose money, and rule number two—never forget rule number one. A great deal of wealth accumulation comes in the form of wealth retention. Given the associated uncertainty, start-ups pose a greater risk of losing wealth.

If you want to live in the gig economy or keep your full-time employment while earning some spare change on a side hustle, then a start-up might be a good fit with your objectives. But that is not what this book is about. This book is about being financially whole and complete, taking control over your time and your life.

Business Ownership through Acquisition

The alternative to starting a company is to buy an existing business—a company that has made it past the start-up phase and has a proven cash flow. By now you will have observed my not-so-subtle bias toward purchasing an existing business.

In order to achieve financial success through business ownership, you have to think both as an entrepreneur and an investor. With the acquisition of an existing business, you are buying:

- a reoccurring revenue stream with a proven history,
- an existing customer base,
- tested and refined products or services that have proven to provide value to the customer base,
- a complete team, including a leadership team and a staff base that understands the operations and is able to maintain customer relationships,
- existing systems, such as ordering, inventory, operations, and accounting, and
- existing vendor relationships.

The end goal is wealth—wealth creation and wealth retention. The problem with a start-up is that it may take two, three, four, five, or 10 years before it starts to see any real money coming in. "You could set up a business using your own money or a bank loan and spend the next few years working 60–80-hour weeks, but still not get anywhere near the lifestyle and wealth you want" (Jay 2019, 7).

Author and self-proclaimed dealmaker Jonathan Jay articulates it best in noting that when buying an established company, "you avoid the stress of setting up a business and taking it through its early development. Someone has already done that for you" (2019, 8). Because "you buy a business that has worked, maybe not as well as it could have, but it has worked for at least five years" (Jay 2019, p 10). You have a proven model.

Someone else has taken it through the early years, has endured the stress and the ulcers, and has missed their children's concerts and soccer games. The business model has been tested and refined, and then refined again. The acquisition story at the opening of this book was of a business that had been in operation for over 10 years. Someone else had struggled through the grind. We achieved with the stoke of a pen what the previous owners had sweated over for a good portion of their working tenure.

Looking at business ownership through the lens of a logical investor, setting aside the potentially emotional lens of an entrepreneur, the proven history of an acquisition exponentially reduces the risk of business ownership when compared to a start-up. This is a good juncture to remember that wealth retention is a significant factor in accumulating wealth.

Businesses become for sale for a number of reasons. Personal reasons include life events such as death, divorce, health, burnout, or retirement. Business reasons include partnership disputes, poor financial performance, liquidation to free up cash, or shedding a division that is not providing synergies to the core business. It is important to understand what the reason is. We will explore that in subsequent sections, primarily that of due diligence and negotiations. For now, understand that there are a lot of businesses for sale.

Entrepreneurs who have spent the past five or 10 years on a start-up tend to burn out. They have put in their time. They underestimated the time, effort, and money that it takes to establish a business. They are tired. This group may achieve annual revenue of, say, a million to a few million dollars. But they are ready to throw in the towel one step before lady luck is about to reward their efforts.

Others may have operated a successful business for years but are ready to retire. The business may have proven to endure, but the owner has moved into coast mode—riding the status quo into retirement. Often, these companies are operating on legacy systems awaiting fresh energy. In either case, this is where you come in.

I have found it to be much easier to double the size and earnings of an existing business than it is to get a new business to that same starting point. The systems and infrastructure are already in place, you just have to add to it. Turn some dials and pull some levers. You have a competent team to dispatch. And you have the cash flow of the business on your side, which is your catalyst for stimulating the growth.

Small businesses trade at a lower valuation (as a multiple of earnings) in relation to midsized and large corporations. This is due to their lack of liquidity and the fact that not everyone is cut out to operate a small business. Therefore, there are more companies for sale than there are serious and qualified buyers.

With publicly traded companies, if you wish to sell, you can do so with the click of a button. Business owners in the middle market, let's say over $25 million in annual sales, for example, also have options not available to small-business owners; they are large enough to attract the interest of private equity firms or larger companies looking to add synergies through vertical or horizontal integration, or they may choose to go public as part of an exit strategy. However, such options are not available to small-business owners.

Additionally, small-business ownership through acquisition remains a hidden gem for other reasons—the allure of the start-up causes many to overlook acquisitions and the work involved with entrepreneurship in general is a further deterrent. Not everyone is cut out to follow through with an acquisition. It takes a lot of time and perseverance to source out the right company to buy and to obtain adequate capital. A lot! Most people quit before they start. It isn't a free ride, but it is often the correct journey.

On the journey to wealth creation, the acquisition accelerates your journey by five or 10 years or more. And time is an important factor in wealth creation. When buying a business, you must think like both an investor and an entrepreneur. This means that you are looking for businesses that have consistent and quantifiable cash flow, each of which are unpredictable with a start-up.

In your negotiations when you buy the company, you ensure that there is an additional return on your capital (and/or the capital of your investors). For example, "if the seller of the business has consistently made $150,000 a year for the last fifteen years, it will be hard for you to lose your shirt unless you completely screw everything up" (Muller 2018, 21).

Aspiring entrepreneurs overlook quantifying the value of their time. With a start-up, it could be months or years (if ever) before the business reaches a level where you are able to pay yourself a compensation on par with what you would have made in the career you are leaving. This is not the case with an acquisition. With an acquisition, you are actively seeking a business with consistent and desirable cash flow.

When you source out a stable company, as the owner you are able to compensate yourself for operating the company from day one in the form of a salary or dividend. This does not occur with a start-up.

Strategies for Growth

Growth through Acquisition

Once you have an established company, whether you started it or acquired it, you will want to grow it. As entrepreneur and *Dragon's Den* co-star Robert Herjavec says, "In business, you are doing one of two things. You are either growing or dying. ... Growth is essential to survival in business, and every business person aiming for ultimate success had better grasp that idea and act accordingly" (Herjavec and Reynolds 2010, 116).

In Allison Maslan's book, *Scale or Fail*, she outlines further reasoning for growth, noting that what "business owners don't realize is that playing it safe leads to unsafe results—missed opportunities, inability to meet demand, lost market-share, flat-to-declining performance, employee unrest and turnover—or, a business that could have been and would have been, yet never made the full commitment to fly, so to speak" (2019, 6-7).

The expenses of your company—rent, payroll, cost of goods sold—may increase at or above inflation. Increasing revenue is required as a basic fundamental to matching this. Team members are more engaged, more productive, and more loyal to companies that grow. They find purpose in being part of that growth.

With growth comes energy, with energy comes innovation, and with innovation comes a further capacity for growth. Your competitors are continually innovating and advancing alternative product solutions to your customer base. They are growing and achieving economies of scale, being able to offer more for less.

It is important that your first company has the right fundamentals—e.g. it is scalable, noncyclical, has a strong reputation, and is in a geographic area where you desire to live—because it is a springboard for your success. In private equity spheres, your first company is called a platform company because the intention is to use this as a base on which to further add acquired companies.

There are two ways to grow: organic growth or growth through acquisition. But ideally, you employ a combination of both strategies. Although few large companies have achieved their scale and level of success without numerous acquisitions along the way, growth through acquisition is often overlooked by small-business owners. Such a strategy can be powerful for small businesses. Once you have an existing business, your platform company, the benefits of growth through acquisition are compounded. This is what we did in the opening story of this book.

You can tack on companies through a strategy of either horizontal or vertical integration. Horizontal integration is the process of acquiring another company that operates primarily at the same level of the supply chain as your existing company—they do what you do. In doing so, you might expand your customer base in terms of geographic reach or by eliminating a competitor.

Often, with horizontal integration, your platform organization learns new ways of doing business, can cherry-pick the best systems and processes from each organization, and roll them out company-wide. Horizontal integration also offers economies of scale and may bring down production and overhead costs, since fixed costs can be allocated over increased revenue. Therefore, the profits and value of the combined companies are greater than the sum of each individual company prior to the acquisition.

Paralleling the Strategies of Organic Growth and Growth through Acquisition

I was recently in a position to examine organic growth against the option of horizontal acquisition. If we spent $2,000 a month on advertising, we would generate about 16 leads and convert four of those leads into new customers. Therefore, it would have cost my company about $500 in advertising to acquire each new customer.

At the same time, we had the option of acquiring a competitor. The purchase price worked out to about $1,000 for each customer under contract.

At first glance, organic growth may have made sense. But the cost of obtaining a customer through organic growth also needs to include the cost of your sales force, of mileage, of administration, and a whole lot of other variables. Most importantly, a dollar today is worth more than a dollar tomorrow. It would have taken us years to get to a level that we could achieve with the stroke of a pen. We chose the acquisition.

When we made the acquisition, staff count was reduced, and two office leases were reduced to one. This brought down our fixed cost as a percentage of revenue. We found processes that they were doing better than we were and some processes where a fresh eye proved the acquired company was operating inefficiently. As a result of this learning curve, customer service across both the existing and the new customer base improved.

Despite completing the acquisition, this did not hinder us from continuing to advertise and to grow organically. Most often, you will want to parallel both strategies.

Vertical integration is the process of acquiring a company that operates at a different level of the supply chain. For example, a manufacturer may purchase a retail outlet, or a large homebuilder may buy a lumberyard. Whether you choose forward or backward vertical integration depends on where you see the greatest advantage—are you securing inputs or creating a customer base?

Some authors have suggested that when you grow through acquisition, the "warnings about overly rapid growth just don't apply because the systems, personnel, and equipment handling the growth are in place in the form of the business you just bought" (Annis and Schine 2015, 17). Well, they do apply, just in a different way and to a lesser extent. You are most likely buying infrastructure in addition to a customer base.

With a platform company already in place, you are now not only attempting to match your abilities to the needs of the target company but trying to match the abilities of your existing business to that of the target company. The talent within your platform company can be taken into consideration in the decision, and you are now considering which elements of your existing organization make it successful, and those "elements of your own strategy, operating model, skill base, human asset profile and strategy, culture and other key building blocks which you are not willing to compromise on" (Moraitis and Keener 2019, 38).

And it becomes easier because your platform company is a springboard for growth. You have cash flow to act as your capital injection and assets as your security to finance the acquisition. And you are no longer alone; you have a team to help assess and to assist with the integration. Your decisions are more fulfilling because they are no longer based in the tens or hundreds of thousands of dollars, but in the millions or tens of millions. It is less lonely, more rewarding, and more fun.

Conglomerate vs. Singular Focus

The alternative to scaling a business (singular focus) is growth through diversification. Some of the most admired companies in the world, and ones that have stood the test of time, are conglomerates.

The strategy of concentric diversification is the process of adding companies that foster synergies between the related companies, whether that be in terms of technology, operations, marketing, etc. For example, a paving company may wish to buy a snow removal company. This would allow them to keep their staff on year around, to use their existing dispatch technologies across both companies, and to provide wider services to the customer base of both companies. Both companies would see synergies from having a common ownership.

The strategy of conglomerate diversification is the process of adding companies simply because they provide a return on capital investment. The search for an acquisition under the strategy of conglomerate diversification is therefore similar to the search for a platform company in that you are looking for certain fundamentals of enduring profit but not concerned with synergies or added value when integrating the acquired company into your existing business.

Successful examples of conglomerates include: The Jim Pattison Group (Canada)—grocery stores, vehicle leasing, agricultural equipment dealerships, media, and advertising, etc; General Electric (US)—aviation, corporate finance, healthcare, renewable energy, etc.; and Tata Group (India)—consulting, information technology, steel, automotive, aerospace and defence, travel and tourism, trading and investment, etc.

A conglomerate model is not reserved solely for large corporations. It is also popular with small-business owners who own multiple franchises: it is easier to oversee multiple businesses because the infrastructure is already in place, and there is a shared responsibility with the franchisor for continually monitoring the market. The policies, procedures, vendor selection, and marketing are the primary responsibility of the franchisor, leaving the franchisee some freedom to focus on multiple endeavours.

The strategy is tempting since the concept of diversification has been ingrained in our minds from financial planners, media, and first-year finance textbooks. However, it is frequently not an option in your first five (or 10 or 15) years of business. You can diversify in your pension, or buy some real estate, but in your first few years of business ownership, your time and money are all eggs in one basket. You will be required to focus on it to make it successful.

"During the start-up, you concentrate on that one basket as if your life (and the life of your firstborn) depends on it. But once you have something that's working and making some money, start looking around quickly for another opportunity. The more baskets the better" (Dennis 2006, 128).

I am not sure who coined the saying that "wealth is built through a singular focus but maintained through diversification." Build a business and go hard at making it work. But set a calendar reminder for some time in the future—whether that is on a cash flow milestone or a timeline of so many years away from retirement—so that you do not ignore diversification, asset preservation, and intergenerational staying power. *Diversification helps the wealthy stay wealthy.*

Flipping a Business

Flipping a business is also a tempting strategy and one employed by many private equity groups. Although this is a viable option for most aspiring small-business owners, it is often misunderstood and mistaken for a short-term strategy. Reality television featuring house flippers has not helped the cause. Flipping a business is not like flipping a house, where you can slap on a coat of paint and stick it back on the market right away.

Businesses have a smaller market of buyers than do houses. When you do find a buyer, the process of due diligence will take a lot of time and effort to prepare the company for sale and to respond to requests. Most requests fall through, as buyers are exploring tens or hundreds of companies simultaneously.

A continuous attempt to sell a company can create anxiety among staff, suppliers, and customers who become uncertain of their long-term relationship with the company. This can cause financial hardship for the owner.

Entering a business with the intention of a quick sale creates a short-term mindset, and whether consciously or subconsciously, decisions are made through a short-term lens. This creates a problem if you give a strong short-term push to ready the business for sale, as it is often detrimental to the long-term sustainability. "Your priorities are out of whack if you're thinking about getting out before you even dive in" (Fried and Hansson 2010, 59). What if the business does not sell in the short-term?

When you have a good thing going, and still have the energy to manage or oversee the business, chances are that you are better off in the long-term by holding onto it. If companies in the range where you are operating sell at, for example, a multiple of three times earnings, if you hold onto it for three more years you would be achieving double the impact on your wealth. You will have the earnings over that period, plus still hold the value of the business in your portfolio. What if you continued to capture the cash flow and increased the value of the company? What if you held it for five more years, 10 more years?

There are reasons for the astute entrepreneur to sell. Perhaps you are in an upmarket and buyers are willing to pay for the short-term record. Another reason to sell is if you are able to take funds that are not performing and place them into a business that will achieve a higher return. Often times, you are better off leveraging the first business as an asset to buy another business and would be better off with both. But there are times where you may see external trends and are less optimistic about your current company and industry over the long-term than you are of the prospects of other opportunities.

PROFILING THE PROFIT POTENTIAL OF AN ACQUISITION

Profile of the Target Company

The easiest way to spiral your life into disrepair is to buy the wrong company. When a business goes wrong, it can bring you down financially and emotionally, wreaking havoc on your personal and professional relationships. It is not like buying a house or a car, where you can put it back on the market instantaneously and have it out of your mind within days or months. Even when you buy a piece of a business through a stock purchase, you have an easy exit.

Yet, buying the right company is the best way to put your finances on a path toward extreme wealth. Buying the right company will be the conduit to achieving your personal definition of success. You may go on to owning and operating it for generations to come. Such a business will be your cash flow, your freedom of time, your wealth accumulator, your success story.

As previously discussed, although this may seem simple on the surface, I have seen really smart people start or acquire the wrong businesses. They had great management skills and processes and worked long hours for many years, but their talents were wasted on the barriers and struggles unique to their chosen business or industry. Sometimes it was because they thought too small, but more fundamentally, it was because they chose the wrong business. I will help guide you through such consideration.

Spend time reflecting on the fundamentals of a target company, and avoid detours that can cost many years of headache and lost opportunity.

It is important not to develop a "fear of missing out" when searching for a business. Warren Buffett repeatedly comments that you only have to be right on the ones that you buy, which means that it is okay to miss out on the ones that are outside your circle of competence to evaluate and to let high-risk opportunities pass you by.

You want a company that is built for the long haul, one that can sustain the test of time.

The pathway to achieving wealth—true wealth, sustainable wealth—is to find an enduring business whereby you are the rightful owner, and in doing so, acquire it for its future cash flow but purchase it based on its historical performance.

There is a lot in that last sentence, so let's break it down a bit.

- You are purchasing an enduring business that you are confident will continue to provide cash flow over an extended period of time. This is in contrast to the alternative of a high-risk, trendy, fashionable, or cyclical business.
- You are the rightful owner of a business when your passion, energy, and abilities are in line with the strategic needs of the organization.
- You do not value a business based on future projections, which may or may not come to fruition. You evaluate a business only to the extent that it has proven to consistently perform in the past. Any future improvements are your additional rewards for sticking to the processes that we discuss in this book.

Throughout the following chapters, we will explore each of these in more depth. We will examine what an enduring business looks like as well as other attributes of a business that are fundamental to accumulating and maintaining wealth. It is important to have an understanding of such principles. They are often overlooked but should be given great consideration before you begin your search for either your first or your next business.

Income Stability for Wealth

Fixed Cost vs. Variable Cost Model

When examining the long-term viability of a business, it is important to understand variable and fixed costs and how they impact a business during growth stages and economic cycles.

Fixed costs are those that do not fluctuate with the level of productivity. For example, occupancy costs, equipment leases, management salaries, or debt service payments tend to be fixed costs. If you are a locksmith operating out of an industrial bay, chances are you can increase productivity by having more technicians driving from house to house without paying more for office space.

Fixed cost models work well when there is a level of certainty in your revenue and when revenues are on the rise. Once a company has scaled the hurdle of breaking even, the cost per unit of production decreases as each unit is produced. The company thereby receives great advantages as it grows and can see substantial return on fixed cost investments.

A fixed cost business model is one in which a company primarily invests in fixed costs—for example, buying a vehicle and not leasing one on a per kilometre basis or paying salary instead of paying hourly or per job completed. When contracts are stable, and the economy is in good shape, there are rewards for operating on a fixed cost model.

However, there are risks associated with this philosophy. Large fixed costs increase the break-even threshold for businesses operating under this model. When sales decrease, companies can quickly find themselves operating at a loss.

An example of this occurred during COVID-19. When revenue dropped for businesses that relied on their storefront—e.g. retail, food service, gyms, etc.—such businesses quickly found themselves in trouble. Pricey commercial rents caused many closures.

A variable cost model is one in which the company's expense structure is composed primarily of variable costs. Variable costs are expenses that vary with the output of the company. Examples can include hourly wages, sales commissions, fuel, or the cost of goods sold (e.g. raw inputs).

An example of a company operating on a variable cost model is a digital marketing firm that draws on contractors to complete tasks, while only being required to pay them for work completed as projects come in. When there is no work to be completed, the company does not have any significant overhead costs.

Although companies operating on a variable cost model may have a higher cost per unit, they are more resilient when confronted with significant drops in revenue. When their revenue decreases, their expenses decrease proportionately. In contrast to businesses with fixed cost models, during economic downturns, businesses operating on a variable model may experience lost revenue but will have a much greater chance of survival.

Companies operating under this model are also better placed to react to changing environmental forces. If customer preferences change, such companies can more easily pivot their offering since they have not locked into expensive fixed assets that are often specialized into a narrow scope of service or that can become obsolete.

It is also more affordable to start or purchase a company operating on a variable cost model, as they tend to have fewer tangible assets. A reduced need for capital may allow you to retain control of your company, as the need for outside capital is reduced.

As you start out, you have the option to rent in lieu of purchasing necessary equipment. However, such businesses will be more difficult to finance, as they have fewer assets for security.

A further advantage is that you, as the owner, are able to grow a business operating on a variable cost model without significant capital injection. If you are able to grow the business without capital injection, it is a better business than the equivalent business that would require a capital injection for growth.

Take the example of the digital marketing firm that may be able to obtain additional customers with added marketing dollars and then service the newly acquired contracts with freelance contractors, only having to pay them as the offsetting revenue comes in. In contrast, a company operating on a fixed cost model would have to invest in significant infrastructure prior to accepting new customers.

When examining potential start-ups or acquisitions it is important to understand the difference between fixed cost and variable cost models. You will run multiple scenarios of different sales levels to see what would happen to net income and cash flow at different levels of increased revenue and of decreased revenue. If a company is operating near its breakeven, it is critical to examine what a decrease in revenue would do to cash flow. The level of risk you inherit will come to light in performing this analysis.

Companies operating on a variable cost model are therefore less susceptible to economic cycles and provide better protection toward wealth retention compared to their fixed cost model counterparts.

Recurring vs. Nonrecurring Revenue

Stability of income is among the most important factors contributing to reduced risk. When examining a target company, or a business plan for a start-up, consideration should be given to the stability of revenue streams. During due diligence of a target acquisition, you will want to determine whether revenues are recurring or nonrecurring/ad hoc.

Recurring revenue provides predictability and stability and tends to come in the form of contracts, subscriptions, or simply through customer loyalty. Nonrecurring revenue is less predictable and thus less reliable.

An example of a nonrecurring revenue is when a company has to continually bid on jobs in order to secure short-term project revenue. If the business must constantly bid on the open market in order to maintain its current revenue base, the organization's revenue, and thus cash flow stream, are constantly at risk.

A key determinant of the value of the portfolio is "the degree to which customers are locked into the current provider, and how likely they are to remain as customers through an acquisition" (Annis and Schine 2015, 45).

To examine the likelihood of customers switching away from your company to another company, you will want to examine a number of factors, including how long they have been purchasing from the company and the extent of switching costs. Switching costs include the costs of cancelling their service with you, searching and sourcing out an alternative provider, examining a new provider's service rating, and signing up with them.

Long-term contracts (provided that they are high-margin contracts) provide more value to the company than short-term contracts or no contract at all, all else being equal. If you have to rebid at frequent intervals, there is a cost to retaining the customer and an ever-present reality of losing the customer.

It is also important in an acquisition to determine where the relationship lies—are customers loyal to the company or to the existing owner? In many small businesses, the owner has remained the face of the company and is the whole sales team. It is not uncommon for customers to be family friends or high school buddies of the owner. If you were to acquire this company, how likely are the customers to stay loyal to an organization run by someone they do not know?

In my most recent acquisition, we undertook an extensive examination of existing contracts, with a specific focus on how long customers had been with the company, where their relationships lie, and the cost—in time and resources—for them to seek out an alternative supplier if they chose to leave us. Most customers had been with the company for quite some time, and their relationship appeared to be with the brand and not with any particular individual. We also determined that the effort to switch was enough to provide a hurdle to switching—not insurmountable but enough to be a deterrent.

In this particular acquisition, we did not lose a single customer in the transition. I find this generally to be the case. However, it is important to make certain you understand the intricacies of each target company, as overlooking such factors that might suggest a reasonable likelihood of customer switching could be financially detrimental to you as the buyer.

Customer Concentration

A number of years back, my business partner and I found a business that we liked listed through a business broker. There were many things that attracted us to the business, including the fact that the company had long-standing relationships with customers from numerous industries, servicing municipalities, developers, landlords, and industrial clients. There were barriers for other companies to enter the industry and to compete with the target company, given that the industry required licensing and extensive safety programs.

During our due diligence, we immediately noticed that one customer made up over 50 percent of the company's revenue. The contract happened to be under tender at the time, but the seller was confident that she could renew at similar or more favourable terms. We built a clause into the contract that she must be able to renew the contract. She was not able to, and we were able to back out of the acquisition.

However, in retrospect, we were quite naïve. Even if she had been able to renew the contract and we took on the business, if we later lost the customer, we would have been left with debt payments and no offsetting revenue. She had a customer, not a business. This was not a formula for wealth retention. Customer concentration matters.

Customer concentration is a measure of how revenue by individual customers is spread across the total revenue base. A low customer concentration occurs when multiple customers each contribute to a small portion of the company's total revenue, whereas a high customer concentration occurs when a small handful of customers make up a large portion of total revenue.

Companies with lower customer concentration are worth more to you due to a decrease in the consequence of flight risk; with high customer concentration, a loss of one or two customers can have a significant impact, if not a crippling effect, on the viability of the business. Although you may find synergies in serving fewer customers—e.g. streamlined communication, deeper relationships—the associated risks often outweigh the benefits.

The risk becomes greater for the buyer acquiring a company than it was for the seller. This is because you likely will have taken on significant debt in order to acquire the company, whereas the previous owner may have been in a better debt position, having owned the company for a number of years and having had the benefit of its cash flow over time. The acquisition loan increases your fixed costs, thus increasing the consequences of any future reduction in revenue.

Although business schools do teach the calculation of a customer concentration ratio, there is no magic formula in assessing acceptable levels. You will be required to use some logic in a risk assessment. What would happen to the company if the largest customer left? What about the top three customers? Would you still be able to manage your fixed costs and still be able to service the debt from the acquisition? Would it still be a valuable investment?

Do not buy a customer, buy a business. Some authors suggest that any individual "customer averaging over 10% of a company's sales is considered a red flag" (Annis and Schine 2015, 242), and the business should be examined with greater caution.

There are several ways to deal with high customer concentration. The first, and often the best course of action, is to not buy the business. Move on in your search.

If customer concentration is notable, but not significant, you might choose to move forward with the business but put in place some safeguards. One option is to have a clawback clause whereby, if the named customer(s) decides to leave or reduce their spending within a certain time frame, the purchase price is reduced. In order for this to work in practice, it is best to either have vendor financing or to ensure enough funds are held back in the form of your lawyer's trust account.

Another strategy for dealing with customer concentration is to have a portion of the purchase price in the form of an earn-out. An earn-out is an agreement whereby a portion of the purchase price is paid out only if the company achieves certain performance targets. Under this arrangement, the seller shares some of the risk-reward.

When selling, the seller's preference is always cash-in-hand. And for most sellers, it will be the first time in their life that they are selling a business. It will be up to you to explain the reasoning that only by accepting some type of earn-out are you able to pay the price you are paying for the business. If the seller does not agree, it means that they, too, fear that their top customers are flight risks. If they cannot be confident in their business, how can you be? Walk away and keep looking.

Seek Stability for Wealth Retention

When searching for businesses, most individuals examine the previous three years of a company's performance. One crucial part of this is an examination of financial performance in the form of an income statement review.

If the business is in a sector that has benefited from a strong economy, a review of such short-term performance may suggest strong financial performance. However, it is important to understand where the business currently sits relative to external forces, such as economic cycles.

If you are evaluating a business based on short-term financial history and the strong financial performance is a by-product of a strong economy, when the economy softens, you will be left attempting to debt service something that you overpaid for. Be sure to consider economic cycles because there will be recessions.

There are many factors to consider in determining how susceptible a company is to the fluctuations of the economy. For example, does the business supply customers—whether business-to-consumer or business-to-business—with products that are essential to them, or does it supply a product that can easily be deferred or eliminated from spending patterns in a soft economy?

Ruback and Yudkoff rightfully note that the "same dip in sales that was merely disruptive for the business's former owner—who has likely operated the company without any debt—may be fatal for you, who will have a considerable amount of borrowed money to return" (2017, 140).

Searchers tend to quickly fall for the allure of a business that has strong cash flow and appears to be a steal of a deal. But the focus should be on the long-term sustainability of the target company. Do not pay for short-term performance. Pay for endurance.

Brian Tracy has noted that in "99 percent of cases where people become wealthy, it is over a long period of time, and it is based on slow, incremental growth as a result of compound interest" (2017, 80). "The fact is that serious money is long-term money. Most wealthy people organize their financial lives in such a way that their net worth increases about 8 to 10 percent per year on the amount of money they have working. They do not look for get-rich-quick schemes or easy money. They are patient, persistent, and farsighted" (Tracy 2017, 70).

The goal is not to make fast money and then lose it shortly after. You are investing for the long-term. Look for a durable competitive advantage. Is this a business that you will want to own 10 years from now? How about intergenerational? The business will look quite different at that time, but will it be one that survives?

A gravitation toward short-term performance is partly why wealth retention is harder than wealth accumulation. It is about a long-term mindset.

A thorough examination of the likelihood that the business will continue to stand the test of time will undoubtedly include consideration of the following: where it sits on the spectrum of fixed cost versus variable cost model, degree of customer concentration, degree of recurring versus nonrecurring revenue, how the organization has demonstrated an ability to withstand economic cycles, where its products are placed relative to consumer trends, and how well the company is situated in being able to react to external trends.

It is therefore important to understand how the company has performed over the long-term and is likely to perform in future downturns. Look for a company that has and will continue to outlive the whims of economic cycles. Wealth is not just about what you make but about what you retain. If you make it quickly, you will most likely lose it just as quickly.

Size Matters

Size of the Target

What is it that you are seeking to achieve through business ownership? What do you require from your relationship with your future company? How much annual cash flow is required to achieve your personal objectives and planned lifestyle?

A clear articulation of your personal objectives of business ownership will help define the size of business you choose to target. Although there are many considerations, at the very least the business must support both your personal compensation and a return on investment.

When deliberating on the size of the business, it is best to use earnings—SDE (Seller's Discretionary Earnings) or EBITDA (Earnings Before Interest, Taxes, Depreciation, and Amortization)—as the defining metric. Such metrics are more in line with owner objectives and provide a normalized approach, facilitating a comparison between companies. Often, people get caught up focusing on gross revenue. However, high revenue does not guarantee that the company is profitable.

The most common scenario for new business owners is that they buy themselves a job—a situation where they purchase a business in which, after they take into account expenses and servicing the debt from the purchase, the cash flow available for disbursement to the owner is significantly less than they would have made by staying in their previous employment.

This occurs quite frequently with storefront businesses such as retail, coffee shops, and quick-service restaurants. But it can also occur with any type of business that is challenging to expand or requires significant capital in order to scale.

The size of the company can vary by your objectives and by the amount of capital that you are able to acquire for the down payment. Harvard professors Ruback and Yudkoff suggest targeting businesses "between $750,000 and $2.0 million in annual pretax profits" (2017, 84) as the best trade-off between affordability and financial reward.

Using similar logic, Aaron Muller notes: "I do not like to buy businesses with annual revenues under $1 million. I learned the hard way that businesses with annual revenues under $1 million are just too small and not set up well enough yet, which means that it takes a lot of effort to grow the business to the point at which a manager can be hired and the owner can become a lifestyle business owner" (2018, 67). Assuming a 10 to 20 percent return, this would translate to a target acquisition with a minimum EBITDA of around $100,000 to $200,000.

The larger the company, the more likely it is that you can achieve economies of scale, whereby expenses as a percentage of sales decrease. The company should either be achieving such benefits or be at the point where any further growth would add significant income to the bottom line for the buyer.

Companies that provide significant earnings will grab the attention of larger companies and private equity groups, which, in turn, demand a greater sales price as a ratio of earnings. Such groups may be strategic buyers, willing to pay higher multiples as they see benefit to the acquisition in fulfilling an overarching strategy. As a first-time buyer, you are buying for the cash flow, not able to capture any particular synergies with other business units, and your purchase price is limited to the realities of the existing profitability.

The size of the company also dictates the role of the owner. I suggest a company large enough to support a general manager or chief executive officer (whatever you wish to call the role), who takes care of the day-to-day. You may fill this role yourself temporarily (whether that be months or a couple of years) or on an ad hoc basis. But if you occupy this role for too long, you will start to focus on the wrong things.

Your role should be strategic in nature. Focus on growth, on processes and systems, on holding your management team to account, on surveillance of the external environment, and on a constant review of your dashboard of leading indicators. If you get caught in the trenches for too long, you become blind to the bigger picture and are not able to provide that external point of view.

The size of the company not only dictates the owner's role but the amount of effort required. Surprisingly, it does not take any more effort to operate a large company than it does a small one. In fact, it often takes less personal sacrifice as a company grows.

With a larger company, the business is able to afford professional management and talent that are able to grow the company for you, and your role becomes one of strategic oversight. You will have a general manager. You will have a sales force and will not hold the primary role of business development yourself. The larger you aim, the greater the likelihood that you are able to hire professional management: someone with stronger operational skills than yourself.

With a small company, you will get bogged down doing the books, taking customer calls, or managing staff. These may all seem productive in the moment, but they do not contribute to the long-term success of the organization or to wealth creation.

A search for a large company takes no more time than for a small one. The larger the company you strive for, the more likely that it can provide you with more organized records for your due diligence investigation. I have walked away from smaller purchases solely because owners could not (or were not willing to) provide accurate historical information in order for me to make an informed purchasing decision.

Eker suggests, "Most people choose to play small. Why? First because of fear. They're scared to death of failure and they're even more frightened of success. Second, people play small because they feel small. They feel unworthy. They don't feel they're good enough or important enough to make a real difference in people's lives" (2005, 74).

Geographic Location

The extent to which location considerations matter in your selection of a business depends on the business and your desired role within the business.

With regard to lifestyle preference, it is imperative to consider where you want to personally reside. Most businesses, especially a start-up or newly acquired business, do not survive an absentee owner.

Even the most hands-off managers still "manage by walking around," engaging with and listening to staff, having a presence, and developing a professional rapport. Even if your objective is to put in place a general manager to oversee operations, you must have a presence, understand the business, and keep a pulse on the health of the business.

It is very challenging to take the temperature of the culture or shifts in culture and morale without a presence. You may eventually shift to working remotely, but with most contemporary businesses, this option is not ideal over the short-term. In a small business, even the most engaged and well-paid managers will not have the same passion for the success of the business as the owner. Having a presence—in your chosen capacity—is necessary for the success of the business.

This may be different for private equity groups that buy significantly larger companies and have an infrastructure of professional management, human resources, morale surveys, and board oversight. But for now, neither you nor I have these luxuries.

Location also has further implications on the economics of the business. For businesses serving the immediate population, do the population and sociodemographic characteristics of the current location bode well for future growth, or does the location provide a cap on expansion?

When my ownership group was in the restaurant industry, a number of our colleagues invested in sites in small oil towns during the boom. In the short-term, such sites achieved record breaking sales. Quick money flowed in, to the envy of all other owners. But in the downturn, these same sites quickly dipped below breakeven, and the money flowed out just as quickly as it had come in.

Before you start your search, spend some time reflecting as well as consulting with your family. Where would you be happy living? Where would you not be happy living? For your first business, this self-examination might result in an elimination of all businesses outside of your hometown. You place a significant limitation on possibilities when you omit the vast majority of otherwise suitable businesses. But it is important to be realistic with your desires and ability to relocate.

Adding Value to a Turnaround Situation

It is not uncommon for distressed companies to be for sale. Although owners initially overvalue such companies, as time goes on, they become more desperate to off-load such problems onto the next owner. The question then becomes should you buy a profitable company with a higher valuation, or should you buy a fixer-upper that can be purchased at a lower price and has the potential for significant gains from improvement?

In earlier sections, I advocated aligning the search criteria for a target business with your personal skills and experiences. This is especially the case with turnaround situations. A turnaround, in this context, is where you purchase an existing business that is either currently losing money or is in steep decline and plan to turn it around into a profitable venture.

During due diligence, you will discover many of the reasons the company is underperforming. Numerous issues are revealed when you have your first discussions with the current owner and understand their management philosophies. Often, owners are unsophisticated; they have taken their business to a certain size, but once it reached that size and they moved from being a doer to a manager, they lacked the skillsets required of the new scope.

Are you able to identify weak operations? Poor customer service? Weak collection practices? Inefficient procedures or inconsistent processes? Outdated or nonexistent marketing programs? There can be significant opportunity in acquiring underperforming businesses.

Although career experiences are important in a turnaround situation, a passion to make it work is even more significant. With a passion for achieving profitability, the answers will eventually come to light. However, the extent of the situation will dictate how much time you are provided.

Turnaround situations can be very rewarding personally as well as financially. Entrepreneurs such as Theo Paphitis have built their careers on acquiring underperforming companies and turning them around.

In his book, *Enter the Dragon*, Paphitis discusses his priorities after purchasing retail giant Ryman from receivership. Recognizing the value of the existing team, he noted, "The first step was to do a lot of reorganizing and to win the hearts and minds of the staff, who were totally demoralised" (2009, 124).

Next, he dealt with suppliers who were owed money by the previous administration, repairing the damaged relationships and further convincing them to continue not only to supply Ryman but to advance further credit terms. He speaks about closing underperforming stores, taking 120 stores down to 87. He then reduced the number of products stocked by the company and rebuilt the way the organization handled its inventory. Paphitis further engaged with the staff, believing that those on the front line are better positioned to articulate what the customers actually desire.

Taking a broader definition of a turnaround situation can include companies that are underperforming, merely inefficient, and losing money but are not nearing receivership or bankruptcy. This space is more aligned with my experiences.

In either case, you turn the company around on paper (an expression I borrow from Paphitis and Stone 2009) prior to turning it around in practice. This will include understanding the inefficiencies and identifying a number of changes, which, once implemented, would increase the profitability of the company.

Such situations fit the personality and energy of many entrepreneurs and resonate with me personally. Like many entrepreneurs, I get bored easily, thrive on the challenge, and demonstrate my value best in turnaround situations. But such traits can also be a downfall, as true entrepreneurship is about perseverance for the long haul.

With any business you purchase, you should intend to add value. You will pay for past performance, but you move forward based on where you feel your personal skills and experiences can add value. However, it is important to be cognizant of where the business sits on the spectrum.

Many experienced business buyers and turnaround agents do not suggest first-time buyers look for turnaround businesses. I advise you to move with caution when the company has negative cash flow or if the past performance shows that the cash flow cannot pay for itself in terms of carrying the debt acquired to purchase the business.

If the company cannot pay for itself, the buyer is left with no room for error and will quickly find themself injecting personal cash to stay afloat. This is not a sustainable approach for most first-time buyers. Remember that the previous owner likely had the business for a while and may have little to no debt.

Keep in mind that, as a first-time buyer, there is a good chance there will be many more skeletons than you are able to discover in the prepurchase due diligence process, which leads to overconfidence in your ability and capacity to ride out the situation. The forces working against you often have more staying power than your cash reserves.

Turnaround situations take immense time, effort, and investment. For this reason, I have found that they work best for strategic buyers who already have a platform company within the same industry. With the benefit of a platform company, you will have access to a support team in which you have knowledge of their capabilities. You can lean on them and thrust them into supporting the turnaround.

If you are already operating within the industry, you are best placed to evaluate the risks, the resources needed, and the time frame required for the turnaround, and you can evaluate through benchmarking where improvements can be made. The existing cash flow from your platform company acts as both your margin of safety as well as the financer of the resources needed for the turnaround.

When purchasing the business, the buyer immediately works toward profitability, either through cost reduction or increased sales, often selling off unessential or underperforming assets. Each product offering, division, process, and employee is examined. The strategic buyer has the ability to find synergies with their existing operations.

Without a platform company, you are examining the worth of the company through a distinctly different lens—you are a financial buyer. As a financial buyer, you must be able to ensure that the company is able to quickly carry its own weight. You do not have the same synergies as a strategic buyer and thus have less room for error.

At the other end of the spectrum is a company with existing profitability. Such purchases still provide opportunity for adding value, as many companies—even profitable ones—are operating on outdated systems. There is opportunity to add value to a company with existing profitability, yet the risk is reduced as the company's own cash flow can be put toward the needed infrastructure, innovation, and growth.

FUNDING YOUR ACQUISITION

Shareholder Partnerships

I used to get annoyed with the old adage that suggests a business partnership is analogous to a marriage. How could a business partnership even begin to parallel such a sacred relationship? But as I get older—and slightly wiser—such a comparison becomes clearer.

What ensures a strong union in marriage? Communication, trust, honesty, shared values, shared vision, commitment, openness, willingness to compromise, shared interests, etc. Such attributes are also found in academic literature on teamwork.

It is therefore important to pick your partners wisely because you will be in bed with them, metaphorically speaking, for many years to come and will likely spend more waking hours with your business partner than you do with your spouse.

For me, the word partnership has been associated with positive experiences. This stems from my personal experiences with partnerships as well as from organizational theory research on teams. In this section, I will highlight the benefits of entering ventures with partners, and more importantly, I will outline some preemptive structure around partnerships that will help to ensure that you not only capture the intended benefits of partnerships but further mitigate the risks associated with them.

Partnerships allow you to enter into opportunities that you would not otherwise have been able to enter on your own. For example, let's suppose that you have actively started looking to acquire your first business and that you have determined that a down payment of $300,000 will be required for the size of the business that you desire. Let's also assume that you have $100,000 in savings but want to ensure that you keep some of it back for contingencies. If you were to have a strict no-partner policy, but were eager to start your entrepreneurial journey, your options might be limited to companies that sell for less, and thus earn less, thereby significantly limiting your purchase options to businesses that are in their infancy—and still unproven—or those that show limited potential.

Personally, I like being part of something bigger than myself, rather than settling for 100 percent of nothing. This is where the role of a money partner comes in, whereby you seek out investors with cash to join in your journey. Using other people's money is quite common and is also advisable.

In an examination of numerous case studies of successful entrepreneurs who had bought a small business, Ruback and Yudkoff noted that none of them "had bought a business before or had significant wealth when they started, and all of them raised money from investors to complete their acquisition" (2017, 5).

Remember, at this point you are unlikely to be rich. The rich become rich by leveraging other people's money. If you can borrow money at five percent and leverage it to make 25 percent, would that be wise? Of course it would, provided you have completed thorough due diligence and prepared yourself for the journey.

One fatal flaw that first-time business owners make is to give away too much ownership and, in a worst-case scenario, give up control. Investors will ask for the world. After all, they are taking on a large amount of (perceived) risk by handing over their hard-earned money and will want a piece of the pie.

To retain control, you need to demonstrate your value to the business and to the partnership. *They may be providing capital, but your time is worth more than their money.* If you have a successful track record (through employment or otherwise) and can demonstrate the value that you bring to the business through a professional business plan, do not lose sight of your own value.

Many new entrepreneurs are so excited to be receiving investments that they undervalue their time and, in turn, give away too much ownership in the business. You are the one bringing the opportunity. You are the one risking your time, and you are the one giving up employment. If they demand too much in terms of ownership, or a return on investment that you cannot support, move on to the next investor.

If you can articulate the quality of the investment to investors, the money will be there. You will have choices. You therefore have the luxury of demanding more out of a money partner than simply a cash injection. Seek out investors who can add long-term value to your journey and to the business. This may come in the form of mentorship, industry contacts, or experience as a successful entrepreneur. You can take the time to find not just a money partner but a strategic partner. If they have these skillsets, and have a vested interest, you now have a valuable resource to help you navigate this journey.

You may also seek out an operational partner—someone who will have a more hands-on role. In this scenario, you are seeking someone who not only brings different skills and experiences to the business but also diversity of thought. If you are good at numbers, they are good with people, and if you are good with marketing, they are good at operations. You want someone who thinks differently and looks at situations through a different lens than yourself. There is little value in a partner who brings to the table the same skills and experiences that you have. You already have those skills.

There is an elevated energy, motivation, and level of accountability within a partnership model. Similar to a project team structure within an office, you have the ability to bounce ideas off one another, to feed off each other's energy, and to keep each other motivated.

Partnerships are also helpful in achieving a culture of accountability. In one of our companies, as the primary operator, I presented a monthly dashboard to the ownership group. A dashboard is a summary of the health of your organization, presented in key performance indicators. I ask the same of operating partners in our other businesses. This ensures transparency and instills confidence within the partnership.

Although I have outlined the benefits of partnerships, it is possible that you do not need a partner. If you can source sufficient financing and obtain the down payment on your own, you might be just fine going in alone.

As a side note, do not risk your last dollar. It is better to use other people's money than to leave yourself in a tight personal situation with no wiggle room. Unanticipated expenses and reduced revenue do arise, even for experienced entrepreneurs.

Depending on the size of the business, you should also be able to hire or inherit talent that offsets any gaps in your personal capabilities. The larger the company, the more likely each function is to be handled by an in-house team and off your plate. If these people are not already in place, the business should be of sufficient size to be able to add such talent.

Extra caution should be taken when giving up ownership to an operating partner. If you can hire such skills without giving up ownership, that is usually the better choice. If you want them to have skin in the game, you can institute incentives that mimic ownership, such as bonus programs.

Thus, if you are able to seek financing and investors who do not require an equity stake and you are able to source talent in the form of employees, you might retain 100 percent of your business. This is a good thing. However, my overarching argument is to dismiss the perception of the disastrous partnerships we all hear about and fear. Do what works for you.

Throughout my entrepreneurial tenure I have been in partnerships, at the ownership level, with about nine different entities, whether with individuals or corporations. I have never had a bad partner. I have, however, experienced how poor planning and lack of role clarity and accountability can lead to catastrophe.

If you take one thing from this section, it should be this: have a clear partnership agreement up front that includes role clarity; that anticipates financial profits and, more importantly, periods of financial losses; and that clearly articulates options for exit strategies. The one time my ownership group neglected to clearly outline the parameters of our relationship with new partners led to the single largest disaster of my entrepreneurial tenure.

After a series of successes in the restaurant business, an opportunity came up to acquire an interest in a number of additional new sites. My existing ownership group was excited to have the opportunity to invest. The partnership had all the makings of success, with the operating partners having been quite successful in the industry. These were very smart people.

However, once we opened the sites, they were subject to both mismanagement and a turn in the economy. Without an agreed upon playbook—in the form of a partnership agreement—we were left on the sidelines as minority investors. We had no clear predetermined path for an exit and no defined benchmarks to hold the operators accountable for performance. This was the short stint during which my net worth dropped significantly.

A partnership agreement would have mitigated such issues. A partnership agreement provides clarity not only for future events but is also a helpful communication document for identifying and clarifying roles and relationships. Without undertaking the effort to document relationships, it is easy for misunderstandings to occur. Partner A may feel that they understand what is expected of them, but partner B may have a very different understanding of what is expected of partner A.

Only through thorough discussion and documentation can otherwise undetected misunderstandings turn into opportunities. The discussions that arise during the process of creating a partnership agreement are as valuable as the agreement itself.

During the excitement of acquiring a new business and the energy of new partnerships, planning for an exit from the business and/or partnership is the farthest thing from people's minds. However, an end—whether harmonious or otherwise—is inevitable at some point. On the personal side, issues including divorce, illness, or death can occur. On the business side, the efforts and commitment of one partner might fade. Plan for these at the start.

A well-drafted partnership agreement will include the following:

- How will the partnership structure share ownership and share class?
- Who has authority to act on behalf of the company? With what limitations?
- Which decisions require unanimous consent?
- What constitutes a majority? Who has the final word?
- How does each party receive their initial and subsequent financial injections back?
- Will cash flow remain in the business or be disbursed to repay shareholder loans?
- Who is to contribute what? How are roles defined? How are contributions measured? And how are individuals held to account?
- How will each party be compensated for their efforts?
- What are the options if a partner wishes to exit the business? Exit the partnership?

- What happens if the business loses money? Who is responsible for injecting further funds?
- How is a dispute among shareholders to be resolved?
- What happens in the event of a shareholder's death?

It is best to have such conversations up front in a proactive and positive fashion than to experience misunderstandings at critical future junctions.

You will also find benefit in monthly ownership calls (or face-to-face meetings, if possible) throughout the length of the partnership. These may be more frequent during the start-up or acquisition and transition phases. Although most relationships start off with strong communication, they tend to experience withdrawal over time or as ventures become "business as usual." However, placing formal structure around communication provides a forum for each partner to voice their input into the direction of the company and to feel that they are heard on current issues.

Financing the Target

Before you search for a company that meets your criteria, you need a plan as to how you will pay for it. A tangible plan (and a plan B, and a plan C, etc.) in advance demonstrates to sellers and to business brokers that you have the ability to follow through with the purchase. A clear understanding of your available capital also allows you to have more control during the negotiations and to act quickly and with confidence when a deal arises.

British multimillionaire Felix Dennis sarcastically suggests that there are six ways of obtaining capital: "You can be given or inherit it; you can steal it; you can win it; you can marry it; you can earn it; you can borrow it" (2006, 71). Although I am still holding out for the fourth option (marry it), for most of us, the purchase of a business will come from a combination of money previously earned and from borrowed funds.

Rich people get rich by using other people's money, borrowing at a lower rate and leveraging it against a higher return investment. Thus, even if you have acquired enough cash to buy a business outright, I would still advise you to borrow a certain amount, ultimately finding an optimal risk-reward balance. If you buy an investment outright, you are not employing any leverage and, therefore, limiting the total return that your funds could otherwise have earned for you. You have a lower cash-on-cash return.

At the other end of the spectrum, high leverage creates added risk and leaves the business, and yourself, vulnerable to any market swings or unforeseen events. Make sure you always have a margin of safety on your journey to wealth.

Some authors have suggested the following as a typical allocation of funds against the purchase price: 40 percent senior loan, 25 percent seller financing, and 35 percent equity from investors (Ruback and Yudkoff 2017); a down payment from the buyer's personal funds of 10–25 percent, a bank loan of 50–80 percent, and seller financing of 10–25 percent (Martinka 2018). Where you land on this spectrum is a personal decision, as well as one dictated by the specific business, the appetite of the investors, the willingness of sellers to carry a portion of the purchase price, and your—and the business's—ability to demonstrate creditworthiness to the bank.

Before approaching banks, it is important to have a clear understanding of their lending criteria. What industries do they serve, and what industries do they not lend to? Do they loan based on assets, cash flow, personal security, personal income, or some other criteria?

You will want to approach many banks and approach them early in your search. They all have their intricacies, and just because you do not fit neatly into the tick boxes at one bank does not mean that you will be rejected at another.

Most traditional banks have a fixation on assets, specifically securable assets. Banks care about one thing—how will they get paid? And if something goes wrong, do they have security against the loan that they can take in the event of a default? They do not care how rosy the upside projections are because they do not share in the upside. They want certainty in the company's and your personal ability to pay.

This is why banks prefer companies with assets. Assets provide security. In this sense, proposals for financing companies in manufacturing or property development, for example—any tangible asset—are more understood by the language of bankers.

Some secondary lenders specialize in lending based on cash flow ratios. These lenders are more comfortable basing their analysis on the historical stability of the cash flow—the company's ability to make the loan payments—and are less fixated on securable assets. Such lenders may even have departments that specialize in your specific industry. I have found such lenders to be very accommodating, as they understand your industry and are more willing to tailor the repayment schedule around the business's cash flow cycles.

In Canada, we have the Canada Small Business Financing Program. Most countries have something similar, which is a financing program meant to stimulate the economy through entrepreneurship. The Business Development Bank of Canada is another financing resource available to entrepreneurs. As a crown corporation, its focus is to support entrepreneurs across all industries.

Traditional banks tend to be the best option for financing companies with assets. If you are purchasing a business that has significant assets, a history of solid cash flow (which is what the goal is), and can demonstrate a strong transition plan, there should not be an issue receiving financing.

Banks will, however, reject loans if the company lacks assets, is unproven, does not have adequate cash flow to service the debt, if you lack what they feel to be a reasonable down payment, or if they have unanswered questions about the credibility of the borrower.

Financing from most types of lenders is approved based on meeting select financial ratios. Ratios will vary depending on the lender, the type of loan, the type of security, the size of business, and many other factors. But the most common covenant is a debt service ratio, which is a calculation of net income divided by debt payments. For example, a loan may be approved based on the bank's confidence in the business maintaining 1.25 net income for every one dollar due in debt payments over the same time period.

Simple loans, backed by security, may have very few covenants, whereas more complex and larger loans may have more complex and multiple targets as well as more in-depth and frequent reporting requirements.

Once the loan is advanced, you will be required to periodically submit financial statements to the bank in order for them to monitor that you are not in default of the required covenants. If you fall below that, the bank will become nervous and place further surveillance or restrictions on your business.

The problem with stringent loans is that if you have an unexpected dip in revenues, the covenants start to operate you and dictate your decisions. Rather than making decisions in the interest of the long-term success of the business, you are forced to make decisions to meet the short-term ratios imposed on you by the bank. For this reason, it is important not only to ensure that you build a margin of safety into your debt, never placing yourself in a tight cash flow position, but that you also understand the lending criteria and whether the lender is friendly to the needs of the business.

Always understand the lender's policy on personal guarantees. The closer I get to retirement, the more resistant I am to signing a personal guarantee. As you evolve, and as your business evolves, the business should stand on its own with credit applications, and the personal security requirement fades into the background. This is especially true with acquisitions as opposed to start-ups.

With an acquisition, the business has a history and can be evaluated against its history. With a start-up, a lot of the lending focus will be on your personal background and net worth. Banks are more likely to require personal guarantees (and your house and everything else as collateral), whereas private lenders may be more lenient on this. Select government programs targeted at small businesses may also allow for limited guarantees.

As you grow as an entrepreneur, financing gets easier. Over time, you quit chasing it, and it starts chasing you. After some time in the restaurant business, countless customers would approach me and ask if we had any opportunities coming up. The public sees your energy and wants to be a part of it. This year, my primary bank, which has rejected my requests for proposals in the past, continues to contact me about their offers. They are offering credit based on my credit history and revolving account balances, even without me applying.

As you continue to develop your businesses, expanding becomes easier because you have a base. This base generates a cash flow that acts as your security, your down payment, and your credibility when speaking with lenders. Your network becomes more comprehensive, and you become known to lenders. Once you are on good terms and have a relationship with a particular lender, going back for more becomes so much easier.

Before applying for funds with any lender, make sure you understand their lending criteria and, in many cases, understand it better than they do. Make sure your application is transparent and complete. Your business plan should outline your experiences and qualifications as well as those of your partners and management. Know what will be required for documentation, such as tax returns, and start to compile them well in advance. Incomplete applications go to the bottom of the pile and will not start your relationship off in the best possible light.

On the personal side, you will most likely be required to submit recent tax returns and a personal net worth statement. I always pull my own credit score in advance to ensure that there are no last-minute surprises. For the business, you will be required to provide historical and interim financial statements (most likely accountant prepared), past tax returns, and a balance sheet with a detailed asset list. Financing for a start-up requires more in-depth business plans and projections. The evaluation of such financing will also rely further on the experience and personal worth of the founder, as the business is still unproven.

Know your ratios. If you know that the bank requires a certain debt service ratio, why would you submit an application that projects lower debt coverage? It will be rejected. Primary lenders are about tick boxes. If you do not meet their tick box, your application will be rejected. At the very least, be able to explain what quick improvements you will make to the business to ensure such ratios are met or apply somewhere else that has a different lending criteria. But most people do not do this because they do not take the time to talk with the bank in advance and understand their lending criteria. Know their criteria, tailor your package to the individual bank, and more importantly, seek out a bank that is friendly to your specific situation.

Most individuals assume that they will not have enough cash to get started. You need not worry; options are available in some combination of bank financing, investor partners, private financing, personal loans, or seller financing. Where there is a will, there is a way. You typically do not need to give away a chunk of the business to partners solely for the purpose of accessing their money. If the business is sound, and you are relentless in your search, there is no reason you will not be able to secure the required capital.

Private Financing Is Often a Friendly Solution

Private money is often overlooked by new entrepreneurs, as they fail to recognize not only that it is an option, but how multifaceted private lending is. Private lending can be in the form of sophisticated investors who provide a structured and formal approval process at one end of the spectrum to borrowing gas money from your grandmother to attend an appointment with a client at the other. Typically, private money falls somewhere in the middle.

There is an abundance of high-net-worth individuals who are frustrated with the stock market and, like you, are intrigued by the work small businesses do. But unlike you, they will complain about their day job until the day they die, yet they will never have the courage to engage with the entrepreneurial grind. Find these people and use their money to benefit the both of you. Once you find them, there is a snowball effect. Rich people know other rich people, and if they invest in you once, they are likely to invest in you again.

I have sought private money for start-ups and acquisitions. One professional services company that we started had very few tangible assets but still had significant start-up costs in the form of legal, office, software, and payroll. This was not something a traditional lender would typically grasp without expecting us to jump through a number of hoops, which would inevitably include personal guarantees. My business partner knew of a friend who was looking to make a better return on his cash and had seen what we had done with our other businesses. With one phone call, and a one-page agreement, we quickly had start-up funds in our account.

Private money may cost more, but it comes with other advantages. You and the lender are able to negotiate mutually beneficial terms and are not limited to the structure and stringent criteria of a traditional bank. For example, I have negotiated grace periods—either no payment or interest only—for a number of months to give the business breathing room during the takeover transition.

Holdbacks, Earn-outs, and Vendor Financing

Regardless of the composition of your financing, it is imperative not to advance the full amount of the purchase price at the time of closing. Holding back a portion of the purchase price—whether in the form of a holdback, earn-out, or vendor financing—provides assurance to the buyer as contingent future events play out.

Your purchase contract will contain numerous terms whereby the seller warrants certain things to be true. For example, the seller may warrant that the financial statements they provided were true. What are your options if such statements prove to be untrue? What if the business is sued for an event that occurred prior to the closing date? In such instances, the purchase contract would allow you to recover any losses that you suffer. But it is a lot easier to negotiate and recover such losses when you have not yet advanced all of the purchase funds.

As a more basic example, almost every transaction will have adjustments at closing, and many adjustments will not be calculable at the time of closing. Late supplier invoices, for example, may not be reconciled until months after closing, at which time money will go back and forth between the buyer and the seller. Holding back a portion of funds allows you more control during such reconciliations.

There are numerous options to provide the buyer with such assurances. A holdback is one such option. A holdback is where the buyer retains a portion of the purchase funds, often in the lawyer's trust account, which will be paid out upon future contingent events.

This is the common method of protection with real estate. For example, in one residential investment property that I was a partner in purchasing, the garage had a lean-to attached to it that was built without the proper permits. We held back a portion of the purchase price until such time that the seller was able to obtain the permits. The seller was unable to fulfill their obligation by a certain date and forfeited the amount held back. Our lawyer then released the trust funds back to us.

An earn-out is another way of satisfying uncertainty in future events and provides for a further option toward financing a portion of the purchase price. "Earn-outs are similar to seller notes in that in these arrangements, part of the sale price is paid on a deferral basis. But in the case of earn-outs, that payment is pegged to company performance" (Ruback and Yudkoff 2017, 194).

An earn-out not only provides a form of financing but also helps to move negotiations forward when the seller has more confidence in certain aspects of the business than the buyer. This can happen, for instance, when the seller has added a new customer that promises to bring in additional revenue, but the buyer is unwilling to increase the purchase price and advance funds based on an unproven revenue source. In such a case, the seller may accept receiving payments over time as certain milestones are achieved (e.g. based on sales, profits, or some other metric). If such agreed upon milestones are not achieved, you as the buyer are not out any funds.

Vender financing (also called seller financing) occurs when the seller of the business accepts payment over time, essentially extending a loan to the buyer to cover a portion of the purchase price. There are many advantages to the buyer in having the seller carry a balance of the purchase price in the form of vendor financing. The most obvious is that it is a form of available financing in a world where you have to jump through numerous hoops to obtain such financing from institutions.

The vendor is in a position to be able to evaluate the company's ability to service the debt over time and is therefore best placed to assess and extend a loan. The amount of vendor financing can vary depending on what the parties choose to negotiate. Although many deals will not contain vendor financing, others will be comprised of a blend of buyer equity, vendor financing, and bank financing.

Vendor financing is more prevalent in deals where banks are apt to be more hesitant—for example, if the business does not have significant assets or the buyer does not have a strong enough personal net worth to secure traditional financing. When a business does not have significant assets, a savvy seller will realize that their prospects for selling the business are enhanced, or only possible, if a certain amount of vendor financing is offered.

Depending on the size of the deal and the type of business, I almost always seek some degree of vendor financing. One acquisition we recently completed had all of the makings of a vender-financing deal. With this acquisition, we purchased cash flow (by taking over customer contracts), and the business was not accompanied by any tangible assets. Banks would have looked at this deal unfavourably, providing limitations for most buyers to come up with the purchase price. It was therefore relatively easy to convince the seller to provide vendor financing—either provide it or risk not being able to sell the business.

By including vendor financing, we were willing and able to pay the seller the asking price. In this example, we obtained 50 percent vendor financing. The purchase price on this acquisition was not a fixed price but a price per contract, which changed day-by-day. Holding back funds in the form of vendor financing provided further protections to us as the buyer in the event that the number of contracts at closing were to be less than estimated.

Vendor financing provides an incentive for the seller to ensure the success of the business, as they continue to have a vested interest. The seller is therefore more likely to provide continued support and make decisions during the transition that align with the long-term success of the company.

Be cautious of businesses where an owner refuses to entertain any type of discussion regarding vendor financing. If a seller does not have confidence in the business's capability to service its debts, why would you as a buyer have confidence in the business? However, such reservations on a seller's part may simply be tied to the fact that they want a clean exit. It is up to you (or their broker) to outline the benefits of vendor financing to them.

Since sellers are not tied to any specific institutional lending criteria, vendor financing can provide flexible payment terms that match the needs of the business. I tend to suggest a grace period of at least three months of either no payments or interest only, which allows the business some breathing room during the transition. The loan will be funded on a promissory note from the business, not from the buyer personally. This means that you are unlikely to be obligated to provide a personal guarantee. Primary lenders may insist that the loan is subordinate to their loans.

PREDEFINED SEARCH CRITERIA AND THE REQUIRED INFRASTRUCTURE

The Search for Wealth

By the time you have reached the formal search process, you will have a clear idea of what you are looking for in a business and the amount of capital available to you from investors and lenders. The acquisition of your first business—and subsequent businesses—is most likely the largest single investment you have ever made. When it goes well, it is a great thing—a life's fulfillment and the start of your journey to intergenerational wealth.

But, there is "also no easy out if you make a mistake and buy the wrong company. If your company fails, you'll likely lose it and all of your savings, as well as any investments you've accepted from friends and family" (Ruback and Yudkoff 2017, 9). If you lose your job, you simply go get another job. But with a business, you are all in. It is for these reasons that I spend so much time in this book outlining what to look for in a company and how to find a company that matches your desires.

This is a good time to introduce the term "aggressively patient." Aggressive means you need to work hard to find a business and aggressively pursue promising leads. You need to persevere in finding sources of financing and in your search for your ticket to wealth. Parallel to this is the seemingly paradoxical, yet more important, characteristic of patience.

You will not be able to buy every business that comes your way, which means that you will inadvertently miss out on some great opportunities. And that is okay. If it does not fit your criteria and does not align with your personal abilities, let it pass you by. The decision is so important that you must be patient in waiting for the right opportunity.

This is a good point to remind ourselves what we are looking for. *The pathway to achieving wealth, true wealth, sustainable wealth, is to find an enduring business whereby you are the rightful owner.* You are purchasing an enduring business in which you have confidence that it will continue to provide cash flow to you over an extended period of time. This is your ticket to wealth.

Have Predefined Search Criterion

Start the search with a clear articulation of what you are looking for. This is a very important step toward keeping you on task. Your criteria must be written down and constantly referred to during the search process. Although it can be a living document, repeatedly updated as you continue to educate yourself during the search process, it is important not to veer from your search principles in an effort to make an otherwise out-of-scope target fit your criteria. This is to protect you from yourself.

I am often guilty of this myself. I put significant effort into defining my criteria based on a depth of experiences and past wins and failures, then when an opportunity comes along that does not fit these criteria, I have a knee-jerk reaction to want to jump on it. It is shiny and new and fell into my lap. This is especially true after a long search. It is only with written rules that I am able to stay grounded and focused on the bigger picture and maintain logic's grasp over emotional whims.

Write your rules in a format that works for you. That may be a checklist, a mission statement, or some type of weighting system. The important thing is that you have the rules front and center, and that they guide your search. They should include the criteria that we talked about in previous sections—such as fixed versus variable cost models, customer concentration tolerance, recurring revenue, stability, and the size of the target.

Clear search criteria will also help you with time management. Among all of the online search platforms, you will come across hundreds, if not thousands, of businesses. You cannot analyze each and every business in depth. Clearly defined search criteria will help you to quickly dismiss businesses that do not meet your objectives and will save you from the impulse of trying to buy a company that will quickly put you into the weeds.

This is especially important when working with investors, business brokers, and creditors; after a series of false alarms, you will be perceived as nothing more than an unfocused tire kicker, and your file will be pushed to the bottom of the pile. Most searchers will not have this level of refinement in their search, so it will help you to stand out and to come across as a professional capable of following through in conversations with business brokers and others in your network.

This Is Not a Quick Process

How long the search takes depends on numerous factors, including the size of the target company, your geographical reach, and other limiting factors. Harvard professors Ruback and Yudkoff suggest that the search "process generally takes between six months and two years of full-time effort" (2107, 33). This is fairly consistent with my experience. A business owner whom you reach out to at the beginning of your search may not initially want to sell but may change their mind over the course of your search as something shifts in their personal or professional life.

However, for most people, full-time effort is not feasible or even necessary. But relentless perseverance is. You will not achieve your goals if searching for a business is a side gig. Develop a project plan that outlines whom you are going to approach and when. How many business brokers operate within your geographical search boundaries? Who in your network would be a good resource? When are networking events held by your local Chamber of Commerce?

I have found two books that do a great job of outlining the search process: Walker Deibel's *Buy Then Build* and Ruback and Yudkoff's *HBR Guide to Buying a Small Business*. It is important to find a search method that works for you, and in order to familiarize yourself with different perspectives, I would encourage you to browse these and/or other books and to speak with individuals who have *successfully* been through the process. The reason that I suggest reading widely and speaking to those who have successfully completed the search and acquisition process is because it is like no other process.

When purchasing a house, you speak with a real estate agent and search the multiple listing service for your area. Sellers are eager to get the highest dollar for their house in the quickest possible time, so there is an incentive for them to scream to the world that their house is for sale.

But the market for selling a business is very different. For most sellers, confidentiality is paramount. They are rightfully nervous of suppliers, customers, or employees becoming aware that the business is for sale. Such stakeholders may become nervous about their future prospects with the company and further exhibit feelings that the owner's loyalty to them has been diminished. For some businesses, this could result in significant financial consequences. As a result, the trading of businesses is a hidden and fragmented market. An effective search is thus one that is able to peek behind many distinct curtains.

It has been noted that only "one in five businesses that are sold are advertised" (Jay 2019, 53). Stated another way, if you focus your search exclusively on the actively listed businesses, "you are missing out on up to 80% of the market" (Martinka 2018, 67). But this is what most people do. Why? Because sitting in an office browsing the internet is easy. They have not taken the time to learn how to search for a business. Between a lack of focused search criteria and a superficial search, most people stop short of bettering their lives through business ownership.

Where Do You Start?

The Search Process

To set yourself apart in your search, you will find benefit in formalizing the process. In addition to your project plan, you will find value in incorporating your holding company early in the search process. Doing this early in the process allows for a number of benefits in terms of professionalism and for legal and accounting purposes. Having an incorporated company demonstrates to stakeholders that you are a serious buyer who is dedicated to buying a business—although you do not need to incorporate to have a company name and to demonstrate legitimacy.

Employing a company name is beneficial if you opt for business cards and/or other marketing material. It is tempting and exciting to spend a lot of time on branding, but keep in mind that your objective at this point is simply professionalism; the branding is for your holding company and will not be a household name. You do not need to overthink it.

Incorporating a company early in the search process allows you to sign letters of intent and purchase agreements in the name of the company. If you are not incorporated at this time, you would be signing them in your personal name with a term in all initial documents allowing you to assign the final purchase agreement to your then incorporated company. It is simply easier, more professional, and requires less explaining in an already busy process if you are prepared early on.

Incorporating early in the search process is also more conducive to including search expenses as deductible expenses for your company's income tax reporting. It is more challenging to justify such tax deductions later on, as the expenses would have occurred in a period when the entity did not exist.

Begin seeking advice from experts during the search process. You will want more detailed guidance from accountants and lawyers than I have provided when you set up your holding company, structure your partnership agreements, deliberate on an asset versus a share sale and as possible support during the due diligence and negotiations phase.

Given the level of market fragmentation, your search will be extensive and multifaceted and will include web searches, networking, working with business brokers, reaching out to your existing contacts, and direct sourcing.

Web Searches

Searching business-for-sale websites is a good resource for familiarizing yourself with what is out there. Each business that you view provides an opportunity to reflect on how it fits with your criteria. There are tons of these sites with businesses in your area, and you can identify them with a quick Google search. The problem with these sites is that they tend to carry the bottom-of-the-barrel listings.

The vast majority of businesses on these sites are the types that constantly seem to be for sale. They are retail, restaurants, quick-service restaurants, nail salons, coffee shops, lawn maintenance, or home-based businesses. They tend to be mom-and-pop type businesses and will not fit your criteria for a number of reasons: too small, cyclical, low barriers to entry, no infrastructure. They are the types of businesses where you are buying a job and making less in compensation than you can make at your day job. There is a reason these businesses are always for sale—because the owners are tired of the grind. They started the wrong business and want out. I am not saying not to look at these sites. Keep up to date, and maybe you will find a gem.

The vast majority of these listings are for sale by owner. For most owners, it will be the first time they have sold a business, so they are therefore naïve to the complexities of the selling process. Without being coached—aka a reality check—by a business broker, they will have inflated expectations of the selling price and will further assume that they will receive the full purchase price in cash upon closing. When selling through a broker, the broker should prepare them for a more realistic valuation and provide them with a list of documents that will be requested by most buyers, making them more prepared for the sale.

Wannapreneurs tend to focus their search exclusively on business-for-sale websites. However, those who engage with multiple platforms and approaches will have a significantly better chance of finding what they are looking for. Increased leads tend to translate into a greater probability of conversion.

Business Brokers Can Assist

Another common search approach is to work with a business broker. The most common arrangement for business brokers is that they hold listings and act on behalf of the seller, and they will have a list of businesses for sale on their websites. There are many benefits to working with business brokers in your search process. Among the most significant advantages are that they not only assist the owner in preparing the business for sale but also ensure that the owner is a serious seller.

Before accepting the seller as a client, business brokers will ensure that the seller is committed to selling. No sale means no commission, so a broker will only take on serious sellers. They should also educate the seller on the sales process, discussing such factors as realistic acquisition pricing, tax implications of a sale, and whether they would consider carrying a portion of the sales price in the form of vendor financing.

The broker will put together a fact sheet that will help you as a prospective buyer in deciding whether to quickly dismiss the company, or whether it meets your criteria on the surface and warrants further exploration. The business broker should also work with the owner to ensure that they are able to provide supporting documents that will be requested during the exploratory and due diligence phase.

When sellers do not use a broker, it is often challenging to persuade them to provide adequate documentation for the buyer to make an informed decision. I have walked away from numerous for sale by owner deals due to not being able to obtain the information that I required for making an informed decision.

Keep in mind who business brokers work for and how they get paid. Business brokers work for the seller and get paid a commission when the deal closes. It is therefore solely your responsibility to ensure that you stay on task with your search criteria and not be persuaded into a business that is not a good fit.

Because they are paid on closing, brokers logically want to focus their time on serious buyers who are capable of closing a deal. Additionally, they want to demonstrate their value to sellers by only introducing qualified buyers. When they list a business for sale, they are inundated with inquiries from wannapreneurs, and their job is to thus screen out the tire kickers from the serious business buyers.

Here you will have an advantage over other buyers in that your elevator pitch is refined, and you are able to present yourself as a serious buyer. Demonstrate your ability to follow through by detailing your research with financing, and make clear that you are committed to buying a business within a short time frame and are ready to execute as soon as you find a business that falls within your search criteria.

Many brokers have also moved toward requesting proof of ability to purchase, which may be in the form of a net worth statement or a copy of select bank accounts. You will also be asked to sign a nondisclosure agreement either for a specific company or a blanket agreement covering any future businesses that they send your way.

Continually follow up. Much like my realtor, we won't speak for months, then the day after I reach out, they happen to have a hot lead for me. Stay top of mind.

A word of caution: in most jurisdictions, brokering a business transaction is not a regulated profession and experience among brokers varies widely. Other professions, such as real estate, insurance, engineering, legal, and accounting, have regulatory bodies and ethical requirements.

I learned this the hard way early in my entrepreneurial tenure, in my late twenties. This is not a story that I like to share, but I will here to help you learn from my mistake. We were examining a company that we liked and placed a deposit of $50,000 with the broker. In the purchase agreement, it was made clear that the deposit was refundable if our conditions were not met. The seller was not able to satisfy our conditions, so we rightfully opted to not move forward with the purchase.

The business broker felt that the seller still owed him commission—whether she actually did or not I do not know—and held our deposit as ransom. If this had been in a regulated industry, such as a real estate transaction, the individual would have lost their licence and been barred from practising. After hearing the costs of litigation and also having empathy for the seller, we chose to split the cost with the seller and move on. In retrospect, we should have fought it to ensure this did not happen to anyone else in the future. Lesson learned: your lawyer is on your team. The broker is not.

Networking Can Bring You Surprise Gems

Targeted networking is a valuable way to let it be known in the private sector that you are in the market for a business. Networking can range from a formal networking event to a casual conversation with your neighbour. Your accountant and lawyer are good sources of knowledge for business acquisitions. Even a small accounting firm will have hundreds of businesses and business owners as their clients. They will have intimate knowledge of owners' objectives with their businesses and the health and life cycle of the businesses.

Every major city has networking events, either in person or through online forums. The local Chamber of Commerce will have monthly events, and local business owners are their captive membership. Be creative in identifying groups that are not exclusive to business owners but coincidentally have business owners and other professionals in their membership base.

Networking is where you will see benefit from your prior planning. Given that conversations are short, your refined elevator pitch and your concise path to business ownership will leave an impression. Given that a lot of people forget your name by the time the handshake is released, business cards are helpful in facilitating follow ups.

With networking and an extensive focus on getting your story out there, you will be surprised by the connections you can make. You may find some surprising sources of private investment or an untraditional partnership that you would have otherwise overlooked.

Direct Sourcing to Owners

A lot of business transactions occur that never hit the open market. It is therefore important not only to network but to engage directly with business owners. There are a great number of baby boomers without a succession plan who would be quite receptive to having a conversation and intrigued by your interest.

Many owners of businesses on the smaller side might not even realize that their business has value and will have planned on turning the lights off on their way out. Such owners, proud of their accomplishments, will be excited to share their thoughts with someone who demonstrates an interest in their life's work.

Although networking may lead you to a handful of owners, you will need to get in front of many more. The more leads that you can secure, the higher the probability of finding the right company sooner rather than later. As with most endeavours, snowballing will be a helpful tactic—ask owners if they know of other owners you could talk to and then ask those owners about more owners and so on.

Professional buyers also use further marketing efforts such as mass mailers, emails, social media, and digital marketing to increase the number of leads during their search. You will find helpful tactics for lead generation in the sales literature or by speaking with people in the sales industry, such as high performing realtors, to learn more about what marketing techniques are currently providing the best return. Drip campaigns may be of benefit in following up with leads, as a business that may not be for sale at the start of your search may come up for sale over time.

Not too long ago, I simultaneously examined two target companies that were both directly sourced from the owners. In one instance, I had purchased a piece of equipment from the owner a year prior, as he was downsizing due to health issues. At that time, we engaged in conversation, I expressed an interest in his company, and we shared some connections in our backgrounds and experiences. Over the year, his health deteriorated, and he was ready to sell. I was the first person he called. After a quick look at the business, it was clear that it was not a good fit for me, and I decided not to proceed with it. But hey, it was a lead, and you need lots of leads before you find one that is the right fit.

At the same time, I was examining another company that would be a great addition to our existing platform company. About six months prior, the owner had phoned asking if I would consider selling our business to him. Both of our companies were at an awkward size, whereby they could barely cover fixed costs and any further growth would add exponentially to net income. We were not looking to sell our company, and I shared with him our growth plans. Months later he phoned again, this time ready to sell his business.

It was a great addition to our company. We added it seamlessly, finding huge savings in payroll, moving two office leases into one, and taking a competitor out of the game. These are both examples of how sharing your story and following up with business owners can provide opportunities.

It is important to constantly be working a pipeline of leads. Do not stop your efforts just because you have a promising candidate. In one search that we completed years ago, our offer, subject to satisfactory completion of due diligence, was based on discretionary earnings provided to us from the broker, which included the amount of the owner's salary for the past number of years. In the due diligence process, it was evident that the numbers were not accurate, nor were the broker and owner able to substantiate them. We revised our offer based on this new information. The sellers did not accept our offer, and we moved on. Even promising deals can and do fall through. If we had stopped our search and focused our energy exclusively on this one deal, we would have been back at square one when it fell through.

The search phase is symbolic of business ownership in many ways. The more you network with people who have been there and done that, the more you will learn. Deals will fall through, giving you a taste of setback, but those who stick with it will close on a business.

Throughout the process, remember to remain focused on your search criteria. Although your goals may vary from time to time, and your search criteria may look different from mine, the end goal is the same. You are purchasing an enduring business that you are confident will continue to provide cash flow to you over time.

Social Distancing from Skeletons

Before discussing or negotiating the purchase price of any business, it is important to know what you are buying—is it the assets or the shares of the company? Although under both structures you will be the proud new owner of a business, each structure derives a distinct series of legal and financial implications.

A share sale is simple to understand. Most businesses that you examine will be held and operated by an incorporated company. With a share sale, ownership of the company would be transferred to you, and you would become the registered holder of the shares. This is similar to the stock market, except that in the stock market you are only buying a piece of the business.

Any ownership of assets, whether tangible or intangible, and assumption of any liabilities follow the company regardless of ownership. As there is no change to the company itself, any commercial leases, customer or vendor contracts, or accounts with tax authorities remain constant, provided such agreements do not contain a change of ownership term.

Sellers will almost always push for a share sale for a number of reasons. A share sale is a cleaner exit and provides financial and legal benefits to the seller. Among the most compelling in Canada is that the owner can take advantage of a lifetime capital gains exemption and is unlikely to have any tax implications on the sale of their first major transaction. The seller also has a cleaner exit, in that all accounts stay with the company, and the owner does not have to continue to manage and close out any accounts.

A buyer should rarely opt for a share sale, as the legal and financial liability remain with the acquired company. Select liabilities are not scary, as they are easy to calculate, and can thus be factored into the price of the business and reconciled at closing. For example, the buyer might agree to accept the accounts payable, payroll liability, accrued income taxes, the business's financing or other debt, warranty, or return liabilities. There may be a benefit to the buyer in accepting these, as they are able to take control over stakeholder relationships and receive a reduced purchase price.

However, other liabilities can be hard to estimate, as they may be either known to the seller but hidden from the buyer or unknown to both the buyer and seller. For example, a lawsuit might arise after closing for an event that occurred under the previous ownership. Such claims follow the company and can cause significant financial or reputational hardship for the buyer. A buyer should always presume that skeletons in the closet exist for established companies.

Every purchase agreement—whether a share or asset purchase—should contain an indemnification term, which provides the buyer with the right to recover any damage or expense occurred as a result. However, the buyer would still have to go through the trouble of attempting to recover any losses from the seller, which may prove unsuccessful. Although certain industries are more prone to liabilities, you must proceed under such presumption regardless of industry.

A buyer should almost always push for an asset sale. With an asset sale, the buyer still takes over the business in full, but does so by taking ownership of individual assets, the brand, contracts, and anything else necessary for the operation of the business. The difference is that the buyer does not take ownership of the shares, but forms their own company, which will be the new owner and operator of the business.

You can either use the holding company that you set up in the search phase to own and operate the new business or elect to set up a new company and have that company owned by your holding company. There are numerous legal and financial implications for both, which has led to different theories and preferences among lawyers and accountants. You should consult your advisory team as to what makes the most sense for your specific situation.

With an asset sale, the buyer has flexibility in negotiating how the purchase price will be allocated among a number of asset classes. Such allocations allow the purchaser to set up new amortization schedules, ultimately taking advantage of depreciation (capital cost allowance) expenses over time. This perk has the potential for significant future tax savings for the buyer.

With a share sale, the buyer does not realize any tax benefits of assets that have already been depreciated below their current market value. This is among the main reasons why a buyer would be willing to pay more for an asset sale than a share sale and why I note that you should know what you are buying before negotiating the price of the acquisition.

Since entrepreneurs are, well, entrepreneurial, it is not uncommon for business owners to muddy their books with expenses that overlap business and personal. For example, the previous owner may have vehicle leases, or a portion of their home utilities in accounts under the company name. In other instances, owners may be operating multiple businesses under one corporate structure.

In my most recent acquisition, the owner operated two brands under the company and also held a number of rental properties. As we were only interested in purchasing one of the brands, the owner was quite agreeable on an asset sale, as a share sale was not practical in this instance.

There are also times when an asset sale is not practical. In one company we examined years ago, the contract with the company's largest customer required the company to maintain certain certifications and licensing, including safety programs. It was not practical for us to obtain all of the required licensing prior to closing, and we additionally feared that an asset sale would cause anxiety amongst the customers and trigger select contracts to go to tender.

Yet another scenario where an asset sale is infeasible is when buying into an existing company, where you are not taking control but investing in an ongoing operation. In such cases, existing shareholders would not see any benefit from the workload and inefficiencies of completing an asset sale, as they would have to essentially undertake a process of selling their proportionate ownership to themselves.

As a buyer, you should be fixated to a fault on purchasing based on an asset sale, only considering a share sale when there are significant benefits to doing so. As a buyer, you would then have to give serious consideration as to whether to move forward and accept the risks associated with a share sale. In any case, a lawyer who focuses on corporate transactions is a must.

Business Valuation

How much should you pay for a business? There is a whole industry dedicated to business valuation, and each industry member will have a different philosophy. A further challenge to valuation is that most businesses sell without being publicly listed. Sales data is held privately between the buyer and seller, in contrast to real estate where a realtor has access to multiple comparisons when pricing a property for sale.

There are many ways to slice and dice the numbers to come up with a valuation. For example, valuators will use terms such as market value, income approach, or asset approach—and numerous calculation methods within each approach. Brokers, valuators, accountants, lawyers, buyers, and sellers will each have their preferred valuation method based on the role they play in the process.

There are numerous practitioner-focused materials on business valuations that provide very in-depth and complex valuation approaches and formulas. For example, see Annis and Schine

(2015) or Holton and Bates (2009) for a discussion of different valuation methods.

I would argue that discounted cash flow is most aligned with wealth accumulation, as it takes a long-term view, adjusts for risk, and considers the time value of money. The discounted cash flow method considers all future net cash flows, both positive and negative (e.g. purchase price, yearly cash flows, potential future sale), while adjusting all net cash flows to today's dollars. This method is also valuable when comparing investment options across differing risk levels and time frames. The resulting analysis is the present value of all future cash flows—which is another way of saying, "If I buy this business, what is the potential impact on my wealth?"

The process of determining discounted cash flow has some complexities and requires the use of a number of educated assumptions, thus it is not widely understood by sellers or business brokers. For these reasons, small- to medium-sized businesses are rarely traded on discounted cash flow. Although I do not have space in this book to perform a deep dive into this method, it would be wise to become familiar with the principles of this precious tool for not only valuing businesses but also for project proposals, equipment purchases, and other investments that your business may make from time to time in the future.

However, business valuation can and should be simple. From a buyer's perspective, you are purchasing a business as a financial buyer and are therefore looking for a company that will provide three things:

- The company will provide you with a salary or be able to cover a salary for a managing director at a fair market rate, whether or not you choose to occupy this post.
- The business will have sufficient cash flow to be able to pay for itself in the form of servicing the debt that you take on to buy the business, with a margin of safety.

- The business will provide a further return for yourself and/ or your investors on the equity portion of the investment.

If a business is reasonably likely to continue to be able to fulfill these three requirements, every other complex valuation formula is simply unnecessary noise. I should emphasize the margin of safety.

The focus of the current text is to provide you with a logical framework for building wealth, not to provide a deep dive into business valuation methods. I will thus focus briefly on the multiple of earnings method, as it aligns well with the buyer's objectives and will provide some general guidance to get you started on looking for your next opportunity. And the reality is that most small businesses trade on a multiple of earnings.

Multiple of Earnings

Small businesses trade in multiples of income, with income being defined as a normalized/adjusted EBITDA (Earnings Before Interest, Taxes, Depreciation, and Amortization) or SDE (Seller's Discretionary Earning). Such metrics most readily define the controllable cash flow of the business and provide a standardized metric that can be used in benchmarking across like businesses.

SDE tends to be the terminology used in smaller businesses, in which an owner occupies the role of managing the company and takes a salary for such efforts. SDE is similar to EBITDA but adjusted by adding back any owner salary or perks that are covered by the business. I prefer the use of EBITDA, leaving in a fair market salary for a managing director, but adding back any nonbusiness-related expenses that the owner has run through the company. This provides potential buyers with as true of a picture as practically possible as to what they would earn if they were to buy the business.

Although some in the industry do not include the manager's salary, I feel that it is imperative to do so; either you will be paying someone to fill this role, or you should consider the amount of compensation available to yourself if you decide to (initially) occupy that role. Sellers and business brokers commonly back out the owners' salary, which naturally inflates the price of the business. Eager first-time business buyers, who simply accept this as normal practice, undervalue their time. By not including it, you risk buying yourself a zero-paying job. Don't do that.

When employing the multiple of earnings method, the value of a small business is determined by multiplying the multiplier by the normalized EBITDA (multiple x normalized EBITDA = purchase price). Small businesses commonly trade on a multiple between 2.5 to 5 times earnings. Where a company falls within this range is based on how attractive it is to a buyer. To be on the upper range, a business would, for example, be stable in earnings, be an asset sale (versus a share sale), not be reliant on the owner, have strong management in place, be larger in size, and have a good reputation, strong prospects for growth, and low customer concentration.

Large publicly traded companies or private equity firms might acquire businesses at much higher multiples, with multiples higher than 15 not being uncommon. They are able to do so due to the fact that they are strategic buyers, not a financial buyer like yourself, in that the acquisition provides synergies or other benefits to either the acquired or acquiring company.

Let's walk through a quick example. Let's say that you find a business with a normalized EBITDA of $250,000. You feel that it has a lot of the characteristics we have discussed throughout this book, making it an attractive business. You are thus willing to purchase it on a multiple of four, making the purchase price of the business $1,000,000. If you were to pay cash for the business, a multiple of four represents a four-year payback. Not bad. But if you are like the rest of us, you do not have an extra mil tucked under your mattress. And even if you did, you would want to employ the power of leverage and seek some level of financing.

The business has significant assets, and you find a bank whose lending criteria aligns with this type of business and offers to finance 75 percent of the purchase price at five percent interest on a five-year loan. You have a private investor putting in 15 percent of the price, let's say at five percent as well for easy math. You put in the remaining $100,000 and have a similar expectation of return as your investor.

Remember, your normalized EBITDA already includes a salary to yourself or to your top employee. Your total payments to the bank and investors equal approximately $204,000, providing $46,000 between taxes, capital upgrades, and the return back to the owner. After the loan is paid off, the full $250,000 EBITDA (minus taxes) is available to you (and your investors)—the proud owner(s)—as a personal return or for reinvestment. Try running examples for a multiple of three, or for a seven-year loan, and you will see more cash immediately available to you as the owner.

It is paramount that you have faith in the financial statements and other data provided by the seller, as they form the basis of your valuation. A lot of small businesses do their own bookkeeping and are unlikely to have audited financial statements. But, at the very least, they should be able to provide financials that have undergone a review engagement by a professional accountant.

The books may also be further muddied with other ventures or discretionary spending that benefits the current owner (e.g. vehicle lease, cell phones, excessive meals and travel, etc.) that are not directly necessary for the operation of the business. There is no easy way to wade through these, other than to use logic as they arise. As the saying goes, "trust but verify." Do not move forward if you are not able to trust the financial statements or if you sense something suspicious and are not able to reconcile the numbers to a level that provides reasonable comfort (more about this in a subsequent chapter).

Regardless of how you value a business, do not lose sight of what the purpose of business ownership is in the first place and how the business will contribute to the accumulation of your wealth. During your evaluation, ensure that the business provides, at a minimum, an income for the top manager, a return for yourself and for investors, and the ability to carry itself by servicing any existing debt you are acquiring as well as the debt obtained for the acquisition.

Although formulas do provide a useful framework, business valuation should be as much about your confidence in the business as it is about detailed valuations. An attractive multiple means nothing if the business is risky. Risk in this case refers to the level of threat to future cash flows, such as a few customers making up a large portion of revenue, unstable revenues, being in a cyclical industry, or a business with a fixed cost model operating close to its break-even point.

Your valuation will be based on past performance of the company. Every seller wants to provide a detailed story about why the business is worth more than historical financial statements suggest. They may even provide you with projections of a rosy future in support of their argument for a higher purchase price. Kindly smile while you attentively listen. But once the seller is out of sight, such analysis can promptly be tossed into the bin. Pay for the past. Buy for the future.

You will pay for past performance but move forward based on your confidence in the magnitude and stability of future cash flow streams and how you feel your personal skills and experiences can add value to the organization.

Negotiating with the Seller

It is important to start the negotiations by undertaking a genuine effort to understand what is important to the other side. A seller's objectives in selling a business are almost always multifaceted, evolving, and often contradictory. Only by understanding what their problems (often called pain points) are can you begin to help solve those problems in a way that is beneficial to both parties.

Actively listen not only to what they are saying but also for the reasons behind why they are saying what they are saying. For example, a seller may wish to obtain a certain price for their business, the knowledge of which is not overly useful on its own. However, if you can understand why that price is important to them, or how they arrived at it, you may be able to find an alternative solution that meets their newly discovered objectives.

Chris Voss, author of *Never Split the Difference*, refers to the concept of tactical empathy as "understanding the feelings and mindset of another in the moment and also hearing what is behind those feelings so you increase your influence in all the moments that follow. It's bringing attention to both the emotional obstacles and the potential pathways to get an agreement done" (Voss and Raz 2016, 52).

Fisher, Ury, and Patton, authors of *Getting to Yes*, similarly note that a "basic fact about negotiation, easy to forget in corporate and international transactions, is that you are dealing not with abstract representatives of the 'other side,' but with human beings. They have emotions, deeply held values, and different backgrounds and viewpoints; and they are unpredictable" (Fisher, Ury, and Patton 2011, 20–21). Get to know who they are, why they are selling, and what is behind what they are saying.

Most negotiations jump straight to discussions of price, which leads to a polarizing and unproductive stance, often straining relationships without any progress toward the purchase. But by taking a more exploratory approach, in which you engage with the seller and really listen to what they are saying, you allow for the discovery of what is important to them other than price.

A year ago, my business partner and I acquired the portfolio of a neighbouring property management company. On our initial calls with the seller, it appeared on the surface that he required a certain price, of which the full amount in cash was required at closing. However, after getting to know the individual better, we were able to dive deeper into his objectives, personal financial goals, his vision for the company, and where he saw opportunity for the new owner.

The seller and I were able to quickly hash out that a main driver was that he wanted to spend more time with his family and that he had become quite fatigued of managing staff and tenants, which was starting to become evident in his client retention and stagnation of growth. Price was not his main driver. He wanted someone to take over who had the capabilities of seeing out his vision. Having now understood this as a pain point, it was a problem that we had a solution to. This knowledge allowed us to focus negotiations on other areas, with the goal of meeting his time frame of not wanting to be bogged down by the business.

By the time we circled back to pricing, we had already found solutions to his problems, so pricing was no longer a fixation, which took the tension off pricing discussions. Calmer heads devised an objective formula toward calculating the price at the date of closing. It was based on industry norms. It was fair. It was objective.

I had a similar experience as the seller of one of our restaurants. The buyer had a system of growth through acquisition and a reputation of being fair. Knowing that there were norms for pricing restaurants, we did not start our negotiations with price. Rather, my main concern was that my team, which I had worked with for the previous 10 years, would be taken care of. It was therefore important to understand the operating philosophy of any potential owners and their reputation for how they treated people. Although this was part of the getting to know each other phase, it was also something that I was able to research through discussions with others who had sold to that group in the past.

By the time we got to price, although important to each side, we had an established relationship, a respect for one another, and an understanding of each other's approach to negotiations. And we had industry norms and precedents to objectively guide our negotiations.

With most forms of negotiation, it is advisable not to make the first offer. Given the complexity of acquisition transactions, such advice is even more important. Until you really dive deep into the other side's motivation, you have no idea which terms are important to them.

I almost made a significant mistake with this a few years back. The owner of a business that I fancied had been speaking about retirement, so I had casually courted him for about a year by simply staying in touch and bouncing ideas back and forth regarding our respective businesses. Knowing that I had an interest in his business, and the capacity to operate it, he approached me out of the blue one day to say his business was for sale and that despite there being a number of interested parties, he would like it to go to me as I would be able to continue with staff and vendor relations.

After we had some casual exchanges about the business for a couple of weeks, I showed up with a written offer, thinking we were at that stage. While my offer—unknown to the seller—was luckily still in my briefcase, the owner proceeded to vocalize his thoughts on what he wanted for the business. It was about half of what I had as a starting offer. The owner was not looking for me to pay for the business in a traditional sense but rather to simply pay for the tools and other assets and for a seemingly random value on top of that—which was not tied to any formula but was simply a number that he desired. Do not force the negotiations with an offer until you understand the objectives of the seller.

Another important distinction when buying a business compared to other more tactical negotiations is the importance of not only maintaining the relationship but of building upon a relationship. This starts by only choosing to deal with people who have integrity and extends to a long-term view of how you would like the relationship to unfold in the years after closing on the transaction.

Taking a combative approach—us versus them—to negotiation runs the risk of harming your relationship with the seller. Negotiating an acquisition is much different than other forms of transactions in that it is simply the start of a long-term relationship. You will want a positive relationship with the seller at every stage of the transaction—from reconciling balances at closing, supporting you during the transition, rallying staff to give you a chance, and, often, acting as a long-term banker in the form of vendor financing.

There are many ways to enhance your relationship. An existing owner will feel that they have significant knowledge to share about how to best operate the business. Ask their advice. Facilitate the feeling of being heard early in the process. Making them feel a part of the process gives them a sense of having a stake in the outcome (Fisher, Ury, and Patton 2011). Such gestures can make the difference in them providing support for the business long after the closing date.

Since relationships are so important in the acquisition process, it is important that you are the lead negotiator—not your lawyer, accountant, or adviser. In the process of selling the aforementioned restaurant, after we had the bulk of the deal completed, we passed the paperwork on to the lawyers to finalize. A lawyer does not have a vested interest in the transaction proceeding smoothly but in protecting you as their client from a risk-mitigation perspective. Once handed off to the lawyers, points of negotiation, which in retrospect were very minor to the overarching intention of the deal, became contentious and put significant risk on the deal not closing at the last minute. Luckily, the buyer and I got on the phone and were able to clear up any misunderstandings, based on our previous intentions and trusting relationship.

I had a similar situation with real estate recently. Until that time, I had a practice of finding properties for sale by owner. Once I'd had a preliminary conversation with the owner to understand their objectives in the sale and what was important to them, I would pass them off to my realtor to present the offer and negotiate the deal.

After a handful of deals that I was interested in did not close for various reasons, I sought mentorship from someone who I knew was closing on multiple properties each month. She told me to try not using a realtor—seek guidance from them where you need them, but negotiate the deal yourself. I then went back to two leads that I thought were dead, revived them, and completed the transactions. In one of the deals, further conversation identified a whole new solution—we formed a partnership. I was focused on identifying the motives behind selling the property and, subsequently, on solving any underlying problems. The realtors were focused too much on the transaction and the price. A realtor would not have had the same level of information on each party's objectives to have been able to identify such a tangent option.

If you ever feel that the negotiations are not going as planned or become combative—an us-versus-you game—take a pause and slow down the process. "If we're too much in a hurry, people can feel as if they're not being heard and we risk undermining the rapport and trust we've built" (Voss and Raz 2016, 30). Take a pause and reflect on why they feel a certain way, and as importantly, reflect on how your stance may be perceived.

Business writer Brian Tracy notes that with negotiation, "the harder you seem to be working to find a way to satisfy the other party (the indirect approach), the more open the other person will be to working to achieve an agreement that is satisfactory to you" (2013, 22). The opposite of this is also true: if you are perceived as not being a problem solver and are only looking out for your own objectives—often at the expense of the other party—the seller will not have a vested interest in seeing you succeed.

Trust but Verify (Due Diligence)

Due diligence is the process of thoroughly investigating the details of the business under contract, both to assess the business as well as to verify the assumptions that you relied on in making your offer. At this point, your offer to purchase will be conditional upon satisfactory completion of due diligence, allowing you time to comb through any documentation necessary to satisfy your opinion of the business.

Although select aspects of due diligence may be performed by your lawyer and accountant, the due diligence process and project plan will still be controlled by yourself. The extent of your investigation will depend on the nature of the business, the size of the transaction, whether it is a share or asset sale, and how well the records of the business are organized.

Before getting overly consumed by the minutia of the exercise, it is important to remain focused on the intention of your investigation, which is to verify factors contributing to the cash flow of the business and to search for any vulnerabilities to future cash flow. From an income perspective, you will verify the legitimacy and accuracy of the income. Does it reconcile with bank statements? Are contracts as you thought? From a risk perspective, are there any pending lawsuits or current litigation? Any environmental risks associated with occupied premises?

You will be diving deep into the intricacies of the business and discovering not only hidden value that you did not realize existed but skeletons as well. Do the skeletons and discovered liabilities place enough risk to future cash flow that the business is no longer a safe prospect, or can such risks be mitigated? Is there a reduced purchase price that will still make the purchase attractive to you?

Note that the extent and nature of the due diligence process is slightly different for an asset purchase than it would be for a share purchase. With an asset purchase, you are one step further removed from the risks associated with any liability resulting from events that occurred prior to closing. But an examination of any liability may also uncover reputational risks.

The table below provides a brief outline of the due diligence process and what to look for at a high level. Your requests are likely to include these items along with a number of others important to the operations and intricacies of the specific business or industry.

Due Diligence Starter Kit

Financial Statements – You will want to examine a minimum of three years of financial statements, including income statements and balance sheets. Also examine more recent statements, such as a rolling three months or six months. A cursory examination of a range longer than three years will be beneficial in understanding business trends and how the business performed over the most recent recession. Are the financial statements audited, reviewed, or are they a notice to reader? Do you trust the information?

Income Statement – Ensure that you have a basic understanding of each line item and that each line item is a reasonable size of expense for the business. Compare year-to-year trends and identify any significant differences that require further discussion. Drill down into anything that does not make sense, as well as into any material general ledger codes such as revenue, payroll, and major expenditures. You will want to understand and adjust for seller discretionary expenses and nonrecurring transactions.

Tax Returns – Do the tax returns match the internal financial statements? Are you able to reconcile the differences? Is there a tax balance owing? What is the value of undepreciated capital cost on the capital cost allowance schedule?

Revenue – Verify what you were previously told about customer concentration. Does it match what you were initially told when you made the offer? Are the terms of customer contracts as discussed? What about customer turnover? Is claimed future revenue actually contracted or simply under tender?

Balance Sheet – Are assets and liabilities as anticipated? You will be doing a verification of assets during due diligence and a general verification of inventory. A further reconciliation and a more detailed verification of inventory will occur at closing. Which assets and liabilities are you purchasing—accounts payable, accounts receivable, bank balances, equipment loans, etc.?

Asset Verification – What assets are included in the purchase? Does each piece of major equipment have a maintenance schedule and a maintenance log? Are the assets as discussed? Do they have a sufficient lifespan left, or will they require replacing? Does the business have titles or receipts to all major assets?

Contingent Liabilities – How does the nature of the business affect the type of events that could have exposed the business to future liabilities, potentially caused by events that occurred before the closing date? Certain manufacturing facilities may contain environmental risks; snow removal is subject to slip and fall lawsuits; property management is subject to tenant claims; retail and distribution may be subject to unrecognized warranties. Where are the vulnerabilities, and how does your lawyer help in protecting you?

Occupancy – Does the lease allow for a change of control? Are there sufficient renewal options so as to not trigger an unexpected relocation?

Employee Records – Does the company primarily use employees or subcontractors? Do key employees wish to stay? Is there any pending employee litigation? Are there unpaid bonuses that have accumulated and will become due in the future?

Every stage of the buying process provides an opportunity to either enhance or deteriorate your relationship with the seller. The due diligence process is no different. Be cognizant of the seller's perception and understanding of the due diligence process. For you, it is (or should be) an emotionless process of investigation. But for the seller, due diligence can be viewed as someone picking apart their life's work and an invasion of their privacy and confidentiality.

When not properly prepped, many sellers do not understand why you require the level of detail that you do. For this reason, it is beneficial to outline in advance the steps of the process—what you will require, when you require it, in what format, and where due diligence will take place. Providing a comprehensive list up front allows the seller to prepare and is viewed as a standard process. Seeking information in an unstructured way and on an ad hoc basis can be perceived as seeking information out of a lack of trust. There will always be follow up requests, but the more comprehensive the initial request the better.

For a seasoned buyer, due diligence is about more than informing the buying decision; it is the start of the transition. Due diligence is a catalyst in building a relationship with the owner and key team members, identifying areas of strength and areas for improvement, and an opportunity to start to plan the transition.

Early in the due diligence process, there is still the possibility of the deal falling through, so you will not want to spend too much time or too many resources planning a transition. But the entrenchment will provide an opportunity to structure your thoughts and provide an outline of the transition, which can be further detailed and properly resourced between due diligence and the date of closing.

The process provides an opportunity to further explore the integrity of the seller. Is this someone that you will be able to work with during the transition? Do you trust the information that they are providing? I have walked away from deals that otherwise appeared to be great purchases when the owner was not able to verify their claims with proper records. Trust but verify. I have also walked away from deals where I had an unsettling feeling about the integrity of the owner. Another common comment from small-business owners is "we made this much, but this is what we tell the tax authority that we make." In any of these cases, run away as fast as you can.

The outcome of the due diligence process might include a go, a no-go decision, or some decision in between. If the findings are within a margin of expectations, you will proceed as agreed. If skeletons are found, are you able to negotiate mitigating or alterative options that still make the purchase attractive? These might include, for example, a price change, an increase in the amount of holdback, removal of assets in poor condition from the purchase, a request that the owner stay on for a longer transition, or an adjustment of the closing date. Use logic and creativity to decide how to account for any unexpected findings.

Too often, eager buyers become so vested in the process that they lose objectivity and try to force a deal to work, regardless of their findings. Moraitis and Keener suggest that loss of objectivity can come either in the form of "deal fever" or "deal momentum." Deal fever is "the process whereby all work is geared toward validating a decision already made by the leadership to buy the company" (Moraitis and Keener 2019, 52) regardless of the findings. And deal momentum is where the buyer has invested so much time in the deal that they start to rationalize away what would otherwise be considered red flags.

Recognize that no existing business with an operational history will be perfect. With any due diligence undertaking, you will find select issues that you had not foreseen, that are unwelcomed, and that pose risk to the future cash flows of the business. It is up to you to determine the extent of such skeletons. Remain focused on whether such deficiencies are great enough to affect your higher purpose of wealth accumulation. Are they simple roadblocks to push through, or do they pose a threat of significant magnitude to your journey?

SYSTEMS FOR SCALING WEALTH

Transition and Operations

You are now the proud owner of a cash-flowing asset! This is your ticket to wealth accumulation. However, your journey is still just beginning.

Although you only valuated the business based on historical earnings, you bought it for future returns, and you want those future earnings to be greater than they were under the previous owners. The next steps in the acquisition of a business are to ensure the organization is operating as efficiently as possible and that systems are in place in preparation for scaling the business for greater profitability.

Only once you have had the opportunity to leverage your skills and abilities into improving the operations can you then move on to scaling the business. There is an old business joke that goes something like this: "We lose money on the sale of every product, but we make it up on volume." The point is that scaling while losing money will just lose more money.

In your first few months, you have the opportunity to examine every facet of the business, from staff morale and empowerment to process efficiency, cost reduction, and untapped revenue opportunities.

The Power of People

I do not recall exactly what I said in my speech that day, but I remember my voice weakening as I went on. As I surveyed my audience, I avoided eye contact with a number of long-term colleagues; I was quite aware that the tears in their eyes would trigger a level of emotion in me that would undoubtedly paralyze me from continuing my words of gratitude. This was me, speaking to our team one week prior to handing over the business to the new ownership team.

We had owned that business for 10 years and had been in the industry even longer. Over my tenure, I had spent many long hours in the business, working side by side with many people that are now lifelong friends. Selling the business was the right decision. I had entered the industry at 24 years old, without any awareness of what an enduring business meant, and without any idea of the concepts in this book. The business had served us well, but it was not a business or industry that belonged on my path to intergenerational wealth. In fact, we had no plans to grow the business, and for the past few years, I had strayed from being the rightful owner. It was time for someone else to unleash its potential.

I always remember this story when transitioning newly acquired businesses. It reminds me of the impact that acquisitions can have on staff and how such events can trigger stress among staff as well as the emotions of the existing owner. Be cognizant of the emotions of others and empathetic in your actions, from negotiations and due diligence through to transition and operations.

Address staff with an openness and with honesty. Address them with unwavering clarity. You may not know all the answers at this point in the transition, and it is acceptable to acknowledge that. But without a continual, open dialogue, every individual in the organization will conjure up their own fictitious scenario, speculating on the worst-case scenarios of layoffs, downsizing, or negative adjustments to factors that affect their work environment or remuneration. "Only once personal concerns have been addressed will people be prepared to take the next step" (Moraitis and Keener 2019, 128). Without clarity, there will not be room in the minds of the teams to allocate space toward the important work.

How you address staff depends on the size of the acquired company and on your intended role within the organization. When taking over large companies, Theo Paphitis claims to walk into the business on the day of the takeover and stand on a chair to address the staff. His speeches are passionate but also contain a forceful dichotomization of "if you don't want to be part of the future, you can go right now" (Paphitis and Stone 2009, 136). Such an aggressive stance is not my approach, and if I attempted such a tactic, it would not come across as authentic.

When leaving the existing general manager in place and taking a behind the scenes role for myself, I tend to direct most communication through the proper channels. However, regardless of your intended role, it is imperative that staff know who you are, that you are approachable and accessible, what your vision is for the organization, how much change there will be, and how their roles will be affected. It is not possible to be inspired to follow an invisible leader.

A common misperception during transitions is that staff and customers are a flight risk, in that the transition triggers staff to dust off their resumes and customers to re-evaluate their commitment to the business. This is not my experience. Provided proper communication, staff thrive on opportunity, engagement, and renewed purpose.

For customers and suppliers, a transition is an excuse to reach out and make a renewed connection between them and your business. It is a chance to build upon the existing relationship.

In our last acquisition, many of the customers had not had direct human contact with our organization for at least six months. The transition provided an opportunity to connect with them, to listen to their suggestions, and to demonstrate that the company cares enough to reach out.

Improving the Business

The answers that lead to almost any solution are already held by the existing team. Theo Paphitis says it best: "I firmly believe that most of the answers to problems people have in business are within the organization itself, and that most of those answers are to be found at a very low level. Head office managers are often far too theoretical and detached from the reality of the business. So a fundamental part of my businesses is talking to the people who work with the customers" (2009, 126). "You don't need to bring in consultants to find out what is wrong with the business—just ask the staff. They'll know the answers" (Paphitis and Stone 2009, 131).

The business was just waiting for you as the new owner to unleash the confined talent through asking naïve questions and empowering the existing team to execute their roles with the efficiency that they wish they could perform.

First and foremost, understand the needs of the business. Are operations already efficient, simply requiring a few tweaks prior to scaling? Or are you in a full turnaround situation, which will require a significant overhaul of systems and culture? Once you take possession of the business, the magnitude of what is going well and of what the challenges are will become clearer. Some of such factors you will have underestimated and some of which you had previously overestimated.

But you should already have a good understanding of the business prior to taking possession. Every step along the way—valuation, negotiation, due diligence, and every informal conversation with existing ownership and management—has been an exploration of the health of the business. You will have already spent months looking at records, talking to the owner, meeting with key staff, and in that time, paralleling it with the preparation of a transition plan. Prior to taking possession, you will already have a clear understanding of the business and have a vision for the future of the company.

Michael Watkins authored a book titled *The First 90 Days*, which studies how a leader can see success during transitional roles. In discussing the first few months of a new job, he suggests that "the actions you take during your first three months in a new job will largely determine whether you succeed or fail" (Watkins 2003, 1) and that "building credibility and securing early wins lay a firm foundation for longer-term success" (Watkins 2003, xi).

Moraitis and Keener similarly suggest that you need to move quickly during integration, noting, "There are numerous reasons for speed, the most important of which is that you have been afforded a license for change. An acquisition brings with it an expectation that things will not be the same. You have a window of opportunity during which, although they may not fully agree with or like the changes you are planning, people from both organizations—yours and the target's—are mentally and emotionally prepared for radical change. The same applies to all other stakeholders …" (2019, 92).

This opportunity is your chance to treat even the most efficient business like a start-up, in that you have a chance to review every system, every form, and every process flow. You can examine contracts that have been renewed without scrutiny, examine product pricing, organizational structure, and the occupancy and lease requirements of the business. Can you shed low-margin products? Is there an opportunity to fire a customer that takes up more resources to serve than their contracts are worth? Are your revenue streams secure and stable? Does customer concentration pose a risk to the stability of revenue streams?

Although every company should be constantly examining its practices and seek to continually reinvent itself, the truth is that established companies of all sizes become more like the Titanic than a speedboat, and a culture of complacency makes it very challenging to continually do a deep dive into organizational practices. The early phase of a transition is your chance to do so. A message of decisive clarity, whether the specifics of which are welcomed or not, reduces stress among organizational staff that arises from the unknown.

Two areas of every business tend to be low-hanging fruit—legacy systems and unrealized revenue streams. By legacy systems, I am referring generally to systems and processes that have become outdated, inefficient, and are no longer providing the best cost-benefit trade-off in comparison to modernized practices or technologies. As you will have targeted a business that has been operating for many years, such businesses are often operated by individuals seeking to retire or who have become fatigued by the daily grind. In either case, their lack of energy toward the business often translates into an acceptance of mediocre performance of such legacy systems.

As Saint-Onge and Chatzkel rightfully note, "When a process is effective, it produces wealth for a company. When it is ineffective, it produces that much less gain, and possibly even a negative outcome" (2009, 39). The ongoing use of legacy systems provides a huge opportunity for you as the new owner to increase future cash flow streams of the business!

Set aside your plan and presuppositions for a moment while you listen to the existing team. But then make the decision for change as soon as you know the answer to that decision. Delays in decisions and implementation, once deferred, perpetuate a culture of mediocracy, allowing the business to continue as it was.

As with any initiative, it is important to prioritize areas for improvement. As the saying goes, "If you have more than three priorities, you have no priorities at all." What are your priorities, how will they be implemented, and how do you plan to track them?

Now What? Scale It!

So now you have your business. Your options are to attempt to maintain the status quo or to grow the business. The issue with maintaining the status quo is that such an option simply does not exist. It is folklore. It is a fairy tale for the reason that to maintain the status quo is to move backward.

What got a company to where it is at today will not be the same practices or philosophy that can move it forward. "Sticking to old habits is a recipe to fail, not scale, and they are no way to live your life, much less run a company" (Maslan 2019, 10). The competitive landscape and customer demand is constantly evolving around you. With current advances in technology, it can be argued that they are moving at as fast a pace as ever.

Playing it safe in business "leads to unsafe results—missed opportunities, inability to meet demand, lost market-share, flat-to-declining performance, employee unrest and turnover—or, a business that could have been and would have been, yet never made the full commitment to fly, so to speak" (Maslan 2019, 6–7).

But because "the scaling process and fear of the unknown and/ or failure are so daunting and scary, business owners are often unwilling to take the leaps necessary to take their businesses to the next level and grow" (Maslan 2019, 6). This is likely why the business came up for sale for you to purchase in the first place. Because the previous owner became exhausted with the grind and feared the unknown, unwilling to take on the seemingly daunting challenge. Without such infrastructure in place, the previous owner was stuck in a rut of performing most functions, constantly bombarded by errors in production, delivery, or customer complaints—each of which could have been resolved by a systematized approach.

The timing of putting in place infrastructure is also a critical factor in your success. It is imperative to put it in place prior to growth, not during or after. This is a difficult concept for many operators who fail to comprehend the importance of planning and thus resist undertaking the significant up-front efforts. However, you need to stay ahead of the growth and plan the systems before you actually need them. Once you need them, once you witness errors in your system, including customer complaints, it is too late. Look at it as short-term pain for long-term gain.

In Michael Gerber's seminal book on taking a systems approach, he refers to the fact that "companies like McDonald's, Federal Express, and Disney didn't end up as mature companies. They started out that way! The people who started them had a totally different perspective about what a business is and why it works" (1995, 68). Act like you are a successful company, and you will grow into your systems.

With growth comes energy, with energy comes innovation, and with innovation comes a further capacity for growth. Your competitors are continually innovating and advancing alternative product solutions to your customer base. They are growing and achieving economies of scale, being able to offer more for less.

In the introductory sections of the book, I outlined the need to define your purpose for wealth accumulation and included time as a primary driving factor for myself. Part of my purpose is to not be shackled to having to perform a certain task at a certain time of day in order to make a wage but rather to have the freedom to plan my own projects and the freedom and flexibility to participate in the activities of my choosing—whether they be reading, writing, travelling, or working on the more productive aspects of my businesses. In order for a business to provide that, it must not only provide a cash flow but a cash flow that is not tied to your individual hourly effort.

Michael Gerber popularized the systems approach as a conduit for growth as well as for removing yourself from the daily minutia, famously noting, "If your business depends on you, you don't own a business—you have a job. And it's the worst job in the world because you're working for a lunatic!" (1995, 40). The presupposition behind this is that you cannot achieve your overarching wealth objectives—however you chose to define them—by remaining an employee in your own business.

Only through scaling your newly acquired business can you scale your wealth. With an eye to wealth retention, it is imperative to prepare the business through a sequence of processes and systems.

Wealth from a business comes in the form of routine cash flow and the proceeds of a potential future sale. Wealth stability comes from building a moat around your company and putting up strategic guards against external forces that could threaten such future cash flow streams. Cash flow can be increased through growth but, just as importantly, must be protected by the same structured systematic approach. Only through such an approach can wealth be retained.

Additionally, the future value of your business is increased and protected if your approach to growth has complied with the approach I present and, as advocated by others, in a way that allows the business to operate without being reliant on yourself or other key players. Only then will a future buyer have the confidence to pay for the value that you have created.

The Typical Approach to Growth Is Flawed

Sales and top-line revenue growth are a hot topic across numerous platforms, and social media feeds are overcome by short courses promising to improve your lead generation and sales skills and help grow your business. Sales skills to help build top-line revenue are of obvious benefit to any organization; however, growth on its own can be a dangerous game and have unintended consequences.

With growth comes a new and different set of challenges. Cash flow is still a challenge—just at a larger scale. Cash is continually required for expansion, for a sales force, and for upgrading equipment and infrastructure. Human Resources is still a challenge—just at a larger scale—as owners panic to embed extra layers to their organizational charts to support the growth. With extra layers of management come new challenges as owners attempt to grasp their new role of motivating indirect reports with whom they have little contact. Such a skill set is different than motivating a smaller cohort of direct reports you interact with daily and with whom you have built up a rapport.

Overhead similarly grows at a rate that outpaces its fair share as a percentage of top-line revenue as extra management, additional office space, and reactive infrastructure are put in place to service such growth. This is all too common. I have witnessed the owners of many profitable companies—restaurants, for example—shoot for growth, only to find themselves with less profit and more stress after an aggressive growth phase—going from owning one restaurant to owning 10, for example.

So why am I advising caution on growth when throughout this book I have been preaching growth? The distinction lies in how one undertakes the process of scaling a company to new heights.

A Systems Approach

In articulating the importance of establishing capacity prior to expanding your business, Justin Goodbread (2019) cleverly refers to the principals spoken in Matthew 7: 25–27, where reference is made to a wise man who built his house on a rock and a foolish man who built his house on the sand. When the rain came down, the floods came, and the winds blew; the house founded on the rock did not fall, but the house built on the sand fell, and great was its fall.

Such systems ensure that while you grow, the following factors remain at the fore:

- Systems facilitate consistency of product or service delivery and reduce errors in process execution.
- Net income does not remain constant or decrease with the growth but increases with efficiencies and economies of scale.
- The business is not reliant on yourself or key staff but on a sequence of replicable processes and systems.
- The business becomes a saleable asset whereby any potential buyers have assurance that the systems provide a safeguard to future cash flows.

With a systematized approach, the "system runs the business. The people run the system" (Gerber 1995, 92). It is therefore the role of the owner and management "to develop those tools and to teach your people how to use them" (Gerber 1995, 101).

It is quite obvious now how systems can prevent errors—a task is completed the same way every time—and a product or service is provided to the customer the exact same way every time.

In working toward my first master's degree, I undertook a yearlong research project that included travelling across Australia, interviewing organizations across various levels of the value chain. The efforts of this yearlong journey led me primarily to the conclusion that consistency trumps quality—something that McDonalds and Tim Hortons have known for many years. Why are Tim Hortons and McDonalds so successful? It certainly is not due to the quality of their coffee or hamburgers!

From a customer perspective, it is because of the predictability of their offering. It should not matter what location you go to, what time of day you arrive, or who happens to be on shift at that particular time—the offering should be the same. The atmosphere is the same, the way you order is the same, and the product tastes the same and has the same texture, smell, and temperature. You know exactly what it will be like before you purchase it.

Business operators who are intentional about each process and the resulting outcome of each process witness success along with their growth. The alternative, which is not uncommon, is operators who let the business happen around them. Although there are multiple ways to document operating procedures, the overarching approach is the same: to plan each step—whether that be customer interaction, hiring procedures, sequence of assembly, or dress code—and document the most desirable way to perform such tasks for your specific organizational goals. Growth then becomes less risky; because it does not matter if you have 10 or 10,000 customers, the process is the same.

Intentional About Growth

The company's workflow processes are then organized around business functions and systems and not around the owner or its key people (Gerber 1995). If a team member were to quit, the business continues without missing a beat. If you as the owner take off for a month—for a vacation or to undertake due diligence on the next venture—the business not only chugs along but continues to grow, all while following the predetermined processes.

A significant portion of this philosophy is also rooted in being able to relinquish control and get out of the trenches, trusting that each task is performed in a way that you have predetermined to be the most effective.

Systems are not just documentation but comprise a plethora of comingled activities and paradigms, including technology, automation, control systems, process audits, culture, and employee support systems. In this sense, every company should consider itself to be a technology company. No matter what your product is, there should be a continual examination of increased efficiency and automation.

In this sense, success in entrepreneurship "has less to do with what's done in a business and more to do with how it's done. The commodity isn't what's important—the way it's delivered is" (Gerber 1995, 73). For example, Amazon is not a bookseller but a technology company with an expertise in automation of distribution. Uber is not a transportation company but a technology company that has harnessed a reliable automation process projected to the world as a software application.

This is why I spent so much focus in earlier chapters on dismissing a fixation on a particular industry when searching for a business. It matters less what you do and more how you do it. Where do your skills lie? Not in cooking, mechanics, or some other job skill but in distribution, sales, or manufacturing automation. It is the latter that will define the success of your company.

"A business can fail in two ways: not surviving beyond its start and not reaching its full potential. While shutdowns receive the most attention, failure to reach full potential is much more catastrophic" (Johnson 2013, 15). Systematize your business as a prerequisite to growth. And only then will you be able to scale your wealth to new heights. Such an approach to growth, controlling every business process, is likened to placing a moat around your wealth, protecting it from external forces.

TAKE OWNERSHIP AND START BUILDING WEALTH TODAY

Take Ownership of Your Journey

There has never been a better time to be an entrepreneur. There has never been a better time to achieve significant intergenerational wealth.

What is holding you back from taking ownership of your own entrepreneurial journey?

Entrepreneurship does not come easy. It takes hard work, perseverance, and an elevated level of stick-with-it-ness. But significant wealth through entrepreneurship is open to anyone willing to engage with the entrepreneurial grind.

If I could tell my 24-year-old self one thing about wealth, I would say: you do not have to take significant risks in order to become wealthy, as substantial wealth can be accumulated through a structured process of incremental gains. You do not have to risk current wealth in order to accumulate further wealth.

Such an overarching philosophy can help to inform many entrepreneurial decisions, from examination of what it means to be an enduring company to deciding between a start-up and an acquisition.

A steady path of incremental gains is rarely risky and focuses on wealth retention in parallel to wealth accumulation. Most of the risks inherent with start-ups are not inherent in an acquisition. With an acquisition, you are buying a proven cash flow stream, and with the practices outlined in this book, you are better able to determine the likelihood of such cash flow streams continuing over time. Skipping the start-up and buying a stable business is thus a safer approach to wealth accumulation.

Entrepreneurship through acquisition can be a gateway to wealth accumulation. And wealth accumulation provides for a number of freedoms, including the ability to take control of your most valuable resource—time.

A strategic and well-thought-out approach to your first acquisition can help you to shortcut past the high risks associated with the start-up and allows you to walk straight into an already cash-flowing business. The steps outlined in this book not only provide for risk mitigation—a safer approach—but also get you there faster, with fewer detours. This does not mean that you leapfrog the hard work. Hard work and perseverance will always be present in your journey. And that is the trade-off of wealth creation.

Your relationship with your time fundamentally shifts when you no longer have to be at a certain place at a certain time in order to receive a paycheque. Entrepreneurship through acquisition can be a gateway toward taking ownership of your time. Ownership of your time is the freedom to be where you want to be, when you want to be there. It is the freedom to choose to spend your time on things that bring the most value to your life.

Find a business of which you are the rightful owner. You are the rightful owner of a business when your passion, energy, and abilities are in line with the strategic needs of the organization. This is where you will find success.

Find a company that has stood the test of time, but one in which the inefficiencies match your abilities and your passion. The existing cash flow of an enduring company paired with the fresh energy of an aspiring entrepreneur is a dynamite combination.

I wish you a faster and safer journey to wealth. Enjoy your journey! Enjoy the grind!

For more information or to connect with the author, visit gregbott.com.

References

Allen, Robert. 2000. *Multiple Streams of Income: How to Generate a Lifetime of Unlimited Wealth.* New York: John Wiley & Sons.

Annis, David, and Gary Schine. 2015. *Strategic Acquisition: A Smarter Way to Grow a Business,* 2nd edition. Bolton: Sandra Publications.

Azoulay, Pierre, Benjamin F. Jones, J. Daniel Kim, and Javier Miranda. 2018. "Research: The Average Age of a Successful Startup Founder Is 45." *Harvard Business Review,* July 11, 2018. https://hbr.org/2018/07/research-the-average-age-of-a-successful-startup-founder-is-45.

Clason, George S. (1926) 2019. *The Richest Man in Babylon.* Reprint, New York: Penguin Random House.

Cumberland, Nigel. 2019. *100 Things Millionaires Do: Little Lessons in Creating Wealth.* London: Nicholas Brealey Publishing.

Dalio, Ray. 2017. *Principles.* New York: Simon & Schuster.

Deibel, Walker. 2018. *Buy Then Build: How Acquisition Entrepreneurs Outsmart the Startup Game.* Lioncrest Publishing.

Dennis, Felix. 2006. *How to Get Rich: One of the World's Greatest Entrepreneurs Shares His Secrets.* New York: Penguin Group.

Dickinson, Arlene. 2013. *All In: You, Your Business, Your Life.* Toronto: HarperCollins Publishers.

———. 2019. *Reinvention: Changing Your Life, Your Career, Your Future.* Toronto: HarperCollins Publishers.

Duckworth, Angela. 2016. *Grit: The Power of Passion and Perseverance.* Toronto: HarperCollins Publishers.

Eker, T. Harv. 2005. *Secrets of the Millionaire Mind: Mastering the Inner Game of Wealth.* New York: HarperCollins Publishers.

Ferriss, Timothy. 2007. *The 4-Hour Work Week: Escape the 9–5, Live Anywhere and Join the New Rich.* Crown Publishers.

Fisher, Roger, William Ury, and Bruce Patton. 2011. *Getting to Yes: Negotiating Agreements without Giving In.* New York: Penguin Books.

Freeland, Chrystia. 2012. *Plutocrats: The Rise of the Global Super-Rich and the Fall of Everyone Else.* New York: The Penguin Press.

Fried, Jason, and David Heinemeier Hansson. 2010. *Rework.* New York: Crown Publishing Group.

Gerber, Michael E. 1995. *The E-Myth Revisited: Why Most Small Businesses Don't Work and What to Do About It.* New York: HarperCollins Publishers.

Goodbread, Justin A. 2019. *The Ultimate Sale: A Financially Simple Guide to Selling a Business for Maximum Profit.* In The Black Publishing.

Herjavec, Robert, and John Lawrence Reynolds. 2010. *Driven: How to Succeed in Business and in Life.* Toronto: HarperCollins Publishers.

Hill, Napoleon. (1937) 1960. *Think & Grow Rich.* Reprint 1983, New York: The Random House Publishing Group. Citations refer to the Random House edition.

Holton, Lisa, and Jim Bates. 2009. *Business Valuation for Dummies.* Hoboken: Wiley Publishing Inc.

Huffington, Arianna. 2014. *Thrive: The Third Metric to Redefining Success and Creating a Life of Well-Being, Wisdom, and Wonder.* New York: Harmony Books.

"Jack Ma." n.d. *Forbes.* Accessed April 7, 2021. https://www. forbes.com/profile/jack-ma/?sh=2af972841ee4.

Jay, Jonathan. 2019. *Business Buying Strategies: How To Buy A Business Without Risking Your Own Capital.* London: The Dealmakers Academy.

Johnson, Kevin D. 2013. *The Entrepreneur Mind: 100 Essential Beliefs, Characteristics, and Habits of Elite Entrepreneurs.* Atlanta: Johnson Media Inc.

Kiyosaki, Robert T. 2017. *Rich Dad Poor Dad: With Updates for Today's World.* Scottsdale: Plata Publishing.

Kuber, Girish. 2015. *The Tatas: How a Family Built a Business and a Nation.* Translated by Vikrant Pande. Noida: HarperCollins Publishers.

Lang, Amanda. 2017. *The Beauty of Discomfort: How What We Avoid Is What We Need.* Toronto: HarperCollins Publishers.

Lee, Suk, and Bob Song, eds. 2016. *Never Give Up: Jack Ma in His Own Words.* Chicago: Royal Collins Publishing Group.

Martinka, John. 2018. *Buying a Business That Makes You Rich: Toss Your Job, Not the Dice.* 2nd Ed. Bolton, ON: John Martinka.

Maslan, Allison. 2019. *Scale or Fail: How to Build Your Dream Team, Explode Your Growth, and Let Your Business Soar.* Hoboken: John Wiley & Sons.

Moraitis, Thras, and Carlos Keener. 2019. *Leading the Deal: The Secret to Successful Acquisition and Integration.* Kent: Urbane Business.

Muller, Aaron. 2018. *The Lifestyle Business Owner: How to Buy a Business, Grow Your Profits, and Make It Run Without You.* New York: Morgan James Publishing.

O'Leary, Kevin. 2011. *Cold Hard Truth: On Business, Money & Life.* Anchor Canada.

Paphitis, Theo and Laurie Stone. 2009. *Enter the Dragon: How I Transformed My Life and How You Can Too.* London: Orion Books.

Pfeffer, Jeffrey, and Robert I. Sutton. 2000. *The Knowing-Doing Gap: How Smart Companies Turn Knowledge into Action.* Boston: Harvard Business School Press.

Reum, Courtney, and Carter Reum. 2018. *Shortcut Your Startup: Speed up Success with Unconventional Advice from the Trenches.* New York: Jeter Publishing.

Ruback, Richard S., and Royce Yudkoff. 2017. *HBR Guide to Buying a Business: Think big, Buy small, Own your own company.* Boston: Harvard Business Review Press.

Saint-Onge, Hubert, and Jay Chatzkel. 2009. *Beyond the Deal: Mergers & Acquisitions that Achieve Breakthrough Performance Gains.* New York: The McGraw-Hill Companies.

Schramm, Carl J. 2018. *Burn the Business Plan: What Great Entrepreneurs Really Do.* New York: Simon & Schuster.

Schroeder, Alice. 2008. *The Snowball: Warren Buffett and the Business of Life.* New York: Bantam Dell.

Schultz, Howard, and Joanne Gordon. 2011. *Onward: How Starbucks Fought for Its Life without Losing Its Soul.* New York: Rodale.

Stanley, Thomas J. 2001. *The Millionaire Mind.* Kansas City: Andrews McMeel Publishing.

Stanley, Thomas J., and William D. Danko. (1996) 2010. *The Millionaire Next Door: The Surprising Secrets of America's Wealthy.* Lanham: Taylor Trade Publishing. Citations refer to the Taylor Trade edition.

Tracy, Brian. 2013. *Negotiation.* New York: American Management Association.

―――. 2017. *Million Dollar Habits: Proven Power Practices to Double & Triple Your Income.* Irvine: Entrepreneur Press.

Voss, Chris, and Tahl Raz. 2016. *Never Split the Difference: Negotiating as If Your Life Depended on It.* New York: HarperCollins Publishers.

Watkins, Michael. 2003. *The First 90 Days: Critical Success Strategies for New Leaders at All Levels.* Boston: Harvard Business School Press.

www.ingramcontent.com/pod-product-compliance
Lightning Source LLC
Chambersburg PA
CBHW031852200326
41597CB00012B/374